THEOSOPHY
AND THE
SECRET DOCTRINE
CONDENSED

THE RACES OF MANKIND

THERE IS NO RELIGION HIGHER THAN TRUTH

by
Dr. Harriet L. Henderson

Theosophy and The Secret Doctrine Condensed
(Includes H.P. Blavatsky: An Outline of
Her Life (© 1909) by Herbert Whyte)
ISBN 1-58509-075-1

Published by

**The Book Tree
Post Office Box 724
Escondido, CA 92033**

INTRODUCTION

The word Theosophy is a combination of two Greek terms, *theos* (God), and *Sophia* (Wisdom), meaning the Wisdom of God, or Divine Wisdom. The word Theosophy was around long before Madame Blavatsky and Colonel Alcott started the Theosophical Society in 1875, but the society was an attempt to put this idea into action.

The Secret Doctrine was a Blavatsky book that became the defining work for Theosophy and the Society, written as a large two volume set. Henderson has taken that larger work and condensed its message down into this smaller and more understandable form. It provides a great outline of Theosophy without having to wade through the larger work, plus includes an overview of the fascinating life of Madame Blavatsky. She was a legendary woman with great psychic abilities and one of the sharpest minds of her time. The second half of this book is filled with her incredible adventures.

A major goal of the Theosophical Society was (and still is) to remind the separate religions of the world that they all come forth from one Divine Being. Religions tend to separate themselves from each other, often stating that they hold a monopoly on the truth and represent the only path to God. This has created strife, suffering, and warfare throughout the centuries. Yet the teachings of most religions are positive, in a spiritual sense. That is what Theosophy focuses on. Sharing what we have in common is more important than focusing on religious or doctrinal differences and a false sense superiority.

The purpose of this book is to provide a clear and brief overview of the goals of Theosophy and to display the life of its colorful and vibrant founder.

Paul Tice

P R E L I M I N A R Y

TO

The Lessons On The Races

We must refer to the Law of Analogy to ourselves and the
Planet on which we live. Our Earth has its Skeleton, the
Rocks that support its Flesh, which is the soil; its circu-
latory system of Fluids is well established, and its nerv-
ous system is one magnificent power of Electric Currents
manifesting its Aura producing evidence at times of peculiar
derangement by explosions volcanic, and severe quakes (quite
human); in all plant life tiny roots shoot out in search of
Life necessary to their advancing growth, drawing theis sus-
tenance from the soil and sun; soon the stem appears putting
forth leaves, buds and blossoms, obeying the higher Law of
Aspiration and thus we expand in consciousness until we can
function on higher planes of life, for we can learn to rise
above the physical, unlocking the door to step out into the
Sunshine of true Life and Knowledge, knowing the world
invisible by the power of our own Soul development.

T H E   R A C E S   O F   M A N K I N D

By

Dr. Harriet L. Henderson

RACE FIRST

Life is a state of existence in which natural functions are or may be performed. And <u>Fire</u> is Life, and Death the origin and end of every material thing. Fohat, the essence of Cosmic electricity or the reproductive power in nature, is the personified vital electric energy or force. In its secondary aspect it is the Solar Spirit, the vital fluid, fine currents of electricity. The Zohar tells that Life is drawn from below and from above the source renewing itself from the essence of Fire, this essence is the Life and Light of the Universe, called God by the orthodox world. In the beginning of Human Life on this planet the only dry land was at the North Pole. The whole Earth otherwise was one vast watery desert and the waters were tepid. Heat is necessary to the action of <u>vital force which is Life</u>, and it is a power far more exalted than either Light, Heat or Electricity, and capable of exerting a controlling power over them all. Continued Life is one constant struggle, on this Earth is only the foot-stool of mankind in its ascension to higher regions, the vestibule to glorious mansions through which a moving crowd forever presses on and on.

In that the Evolution of Mankind the Secret Doctrine postulates three new propositions which stand in direct antagonism to Modern Science as well as to current religious dogmas.

First -- it teaches the simultaneous evolution of seven human Groups on seven different portions of the Globe.

Second -- the birth of the Astral before the physical body, the former being the pattern.

Third -- that man preceded every mammalian (the anthropoids included). In the animal kingdom, Genesis 11, 7, Adam is formed. And verse 19 says "out of the ground the Lord God formed every beast of the field and every fowl of the air, and brought them unto Adam to see what he would call them." Thus man was created before the animals, for the animals mentioned in <u>Chapter first</u> are the <u>Signs of the Zodiac</u>.

While the man male and female is not man, but the host of forces or Angels made in God's image and after his likeness, and Adam man is not made in the likeness nor is it so asserted.

The second Adam is esoterically a septonary which represents seven groups of men - Adam Kadmon.

The first is the synthesis of the ten Sephiroth. Of these the upper triad remains in the Archetypal world as the future trinity, while the seven lower create a material manifested world, and this septemate is the second Adam (Apron - Masonic).

The mysteries upon which Genesis was fabricated came from Egypt. The God of the first chapter is the Logos. And the Lord God of the second chapter, the Creative Elohim, the lower powers.

The first continent or first terra firma on which the First Race was evolved by Divine Progenitors was called the imperishable sacred land; the reason for this name was that this continent never shared the fate of the others, its destiny was to last from the beginning, to the end of the Manvantara throughout each Round. It is the cradle of the first Man and the dwelling of the last divine mortal chosen as a Shista (i.e., the Sages, or Celestial Ancestors), the seed of the next Humanity.

Of this mysterious and sacred land very little can be said except that the Pole Star has its watchful eye upon it from the dawn to the close of the twilight of a day of the Great Breath.

The second continent, or home of the Second Race was called Hyperborean; it comprised the whole of that which is now known as Northern Asia. It knew no winter in those days, nor have its sorry remains more than one night and day during the day even now.

The first creation of men were empty shadows, corresponding to the shadowing forth of form in the protoplasm of Embryonic Life in Utero.

The Creators are perplexed how to create a thinking man, for mind is the treasure of the Universe. What is needed for the formation of perfect man? The first process of the Evolution of Mankind is far easier to accept than the one which follows it. An Adam made of the dust of the ground will always be found preferable by a certain class of students to one projected out of the ethereal body of his creator. But very soon the day will dawn when the world must choose whether it will accept the miraculous creation of man (and Kosmos also) out of nothing according to the dead letter of Genesis.

The evolution from the ape kingdom, or the logical teaching of Occult Philosophy, that the first human stock was projected by higher and semi-divine beings out of their own essence - as above so below - correspondence here must be inferred. Man was not created the complete being he is now, however imperfect he still remains. There was a spiritual, a psychic, an intellectual and an animal evolution from the highest to lowest, as well as a physical development from the simple and homogenious up to the more complex and heterogeneous. This double evolution in two contrary directions required various ages of divers natures and degrees of spirituality and intellectuality to fabricate the being now known as man.

The one ever active inerring Law furnishes an ascending scale for the manifested great illusion plunging spirits deeper and deeper into materiality, and then redeeming and liberating it through flesh. And this Law uses for these purposes, Beings from other and higher planes; men or minds in accordance with their Karmic necessities, and their ancestors or fashioners were identical with those possessed of the physical Creative Fire. They could only create, or rather clothe, the human monads with their own Astral selves. They could not make man in their image and likeness. Man must not be like one of us, say the creative Gods entrusted with the fabrication of the lower animal, but higher.

This means, esoterically, that creating out of their own divine essence it is they who became the First Race and thus shared its destiny and further evolution. They could not give to man that sacred Spark which burns and expands into the flower of human reason and self-consciousness (i.e. mind and soul) for they had it not to give. This was left to that class of Devas who became symbolized in Greece under the name of Prometheus. They had naught to do with the physical body, yet everything with the purely spiritual man. Each class of Creators endows man with what he has to give; the one builds his external form; the other gives him its essence, which later on becomes the human Higher Self owing to the personal exertion of the Individual. But they could not make men as they were themselves perfect because sinless; and they were sinless because having only the first pale shadow outlines of attributes and these all perfect from the human standpoint, while pure and cold as the virgin snow. Where there is no struggle there is no merit.

Humanity of the Earth earthy, was not destined to be created by the Angels of the first Divine Breath. Therefore they are said to have refused to create, and man had to be formed by more material creators who in their turn could give no more than what they had in their own Nature to give.

The first Humanity were a pale copy of their progenitors: less ethereal and spiritual, less divine and perfect than themselves - only shadowy men. (A correspondence is found in the early embryo). We now refer to vague and mystic statements from the Old Book of Dzyan. The first were Sons of Yoga. Their Sons the children of the Yellow Father and White Mother (i.e. - Sun and Moon).

The Second Race was the product of budding and expansion, and A-Sexual from the Sexless. Thus, O Lanoo, was the second Race produced; their Fathers were the Self-born, the Chhaya from the brilliant Bodies of the Lords, the Fathers the Sons of Twilight. (shaded - obscure).

When the Race became old, the old waters mixed with the fresher waters, when its drops became turbid they vanished and disappeared in the new stream, the hot stream of life; the outer of the first became the inner of the second. Every Race in its evolution is said to be born under the direct influence of one of the Planets, i.e., its spiritual meaning.

The first Race received its breath of Life from the Sun, while the Third, who fell into Generation, separating from Androgyne into separate entities, Male and Female, is said to be under the direct influence of Venus, the little Sun in which the Solar Orb stores his Light. Science teaches that Venus receives from the Sun twice as much Light and heat as the Earth, thus this Planet, precurser of the dawn and the twilight, the most radiant of all the Planets, is said to give the Earth one third of the supply she receives and has two parts left for herself. This has an Occult as well as an Astronomical meaning. Our whole Earth has been convulsed periodically and since the appearance of the First Race four times; each time the whole face of the Earth was transformed excepting the Poles, they were but little altered. The Polar lands unite and break off from each other into islands and peninsulas, yet remain ever the same (or the Head) and the Antarctic, the ever living and concealed (the Heart), while the Mediterranean, Atlantic, Pacific and other regions disappear and re-appear in turn into and above the great Waters.

The First Race had niether type or color (White), and a hardly objective though colossal form. Mankind was born at the North end of our globe on the only dry land of that beginning of the Races (or life): it was there motion-less and the whole earth from there was one watery desert and the waters were tepid; (Heat is required for generation) there was eternal spring in darkness, but that which is darkness to the man of today was light to the man of his dawn. There the Gods rested, and Fohat reigns ever since.

The literal meaning of Fohat is "Son of the Waters", but these waters are not the liquid we know, but an ether, the Fiery waters of space. Fohat is the Son of Ether and is also the Light of the Logos.

In the first beginning of human lkie the only dry land was at the North Pole. Between the First and Second Races the eternal central land was divided by the Waters of Life (i.e. animating Fohat). It animates the body of Mother Earth. Its one issue from her head. It becomes foul at her feet (i.e. South Pole): it is purified when returned to her Heart which beats under the foot of the sacred Shambalah, an island in the Gobi desert, which in the beginning was not yet born for it is in the belt of man's dwelling (the Earth) that lies con-cealed the life and health of all that lives and breathes.

During the First and Second Races the belt was covered with the great wat-ers, but the great Mother traveled under the waves and a new land was born, joined to the first one which our wise men call the head-gear or Cap. She traveled harder for the Third Race and her waist and havel appeared above the water. It was the belt of the sacred Himavat (i.e., Himalayas) which stretches around the world. She broke toward the setting sun from the neck downward (i.e. South West). (Note symbology of Masonry - South and West Gate). Into many lands and islands, but the Eternal Land (the Cap) broke not asunder. Dry lands covered the face of the Silent Waters to the four sides of the world. All these perished in their turn, then appeared the abode of the wicked (Atlantis). The Eternal Land was now hid for the water became solid (frozen) under the breath of her nostrils (i.e., power of magnetism), and the evil minds from the Dragon's mouth.

The first continent of the First Race exists to this day and will prevail to the end. Most of Asia issued from under the waters after the destruction of Atlantis. Africa came later, Europe being the fifth and latest continent. Portions of the two Americas being far older.

Atlantis appeared as the fourth continent but was the third to disappear. The continents perish in turn by Fire and Water, through earthquakes and volcanic eruptions or by sinking, and the great displacement of waters.

The First Race were Chahayas (shadows), the second the sweatborn. The Third the Egg born and the holy Fathers born by the power of Krivashakti. The Fourth were the children of the Padmapadami (the Chenrisi), the Divine Avalo-kiteswara or on-looking Lord. The First Race had three elements but no living fire; they were ethereal non-intelligent but super-spiritual, and the phenomena of this sexless, mindless Race was that instead of dying, it disappeared in the Second Race, as certain lower lives and plants do in their progeny. It was a wholesale transformation; the First because the Second Root RACE without either begetting it, procreating it, or dying; they passed by together as it is writ-ten. The body of the First Race was devoid of all understanding (mind, intel-ligence, and will). The inner being the Higher Self though within the earthly frame was unconnected with it - the link of the Manas was not yet there.

From the First emanated the Second, called the Sweat-born, the homeless. The First were the Sons of Yoga; their Sons the children of the Yellow Father and the White Mother - Sun and Moon. The nursling of the ether or the Wind (?); they were shadows of the shadows of the Lords. The shadows expanded, the Spi-rits of the Earth clothed them, the Solar Lhas warmed them, i.e. preserved the vital fire in the nascent physical form; the Breath had Life but no understand-ing (Infant in Utero); they had no Fire or Water of their own - the Father the Sun, its Mother the Moon; the Wind carries it in his bosom and the nurse is the spirituous Earth. The spiritual Fire instructor. This Fire is the Higher Self, the Spiritual Ego, that which reincarnates under the influence of its lower personal selves changing with every rebirth full of Tanha, or desire to live. It is a strange Law of Nature that on this plane the higher spiritual nature should be, so to say, in bondage to the lower. Unless the Ego takes refuge in all spirit and merges entirely into the essence thereof, the personal Ego may goad it to the bitter end.

The First Race was speechless, the Second had a chant like the sound lang-uage. As soon as man was created everything was complete, including the upper and nether worlds - for everything is comprised in man; he unites in himself all forms. (Divine Geometry). But this does not relate to our degenerated mankind; it is only occasionally that men are born who are the types that men should be, but what as yet he is not.

The First Races of men were spiritual, their protoplastic bodies were not composed of the gross and material substances of which we see them composed today. The First men were created with all the faculties of the Deity and powers for transcending those of the Angelic host; they were the direct eman-ations from the Macrocosm, while present humanity is even several degrees re-moved from the earthly Adam who was the Microcosm. Mankind was intended from the first to be a being of both progress and retrogressive nature. Beginning at the apex of the Divine Cycle he gradually began receding from the center of Light, acquiring at every new and lower sphere of being a more solid physical form and losing a portion of his divine faculties. In the fall we see simply the law of the dual evolution. The career of Race existences began by dwelling in the Garden of Eden dressed in the Celestial Garment which is a garment of heavenly light. But when expelled from Eden they were clothed with coats of skin under the law of necessary evolution.

But even on this earth the material degradation in which the divine spark was to begin its physical progression in a series of imprisonments, if we but exercise our will and call the divine to our ade, mankind can transcend the powers of the Angels.

The mystery of the earthly man is after the mystery of the Heavenly Man. The wise can read the mysteries in the human face (i.e. the openings and their functions) and since the time of man's separation from its Celestial Garment of Heavenly Light, its quest has been to again come in touch and be cognizent of that luminous body (i.e. the Masonic search for Light). It is the long sought goal of all secret Fraternities, and from the very day when the mystic found the means of communication between this world and the world of the invisible host between the sphere of matter and that of pure spirit he concluded that to abandon this mysterious science to the profanation of the rabble was to lose it. Abuse of it might lead mankind to speedy destruction.

The first self-made Adept initiated but a select few and kept silence with the multitudes; he recognized his God and felt the great being within himself; then, like Socrates, he could repeat to himself as well as to his fellow men: "O Man, know thyself" for thus he succeeded in recognizing his God within himself. And we cannot attain the kingdom of Heaven unless we unite ourselves indissolubly with our Lord of Light and Splendor - our Immortal God. It is by analogy that we learn the Truth of Light and Law.

In studying the creation of the human embryo we learn that Life precedes form and life survives the last atom, the life-thread running through successive generations.

It does not seem unnatural or supernatural to us when we consider the process of the growth and development of an atom, then an Embryo into a healthy Baby weighing several pounds, evolving from the segmentation of an infinitesimally small ovum and spermatazoon. And afterwards we see the body develop into a six foot man. This is Atomic and Physical expansion from the unseen to the visible, and science has never yet been able to name the forces at work in the formation of this marvelous structure and the cause of hereditary transmission. Neither will they ever be able to do so until scientists condescend to accept the Occult theories. But when this marvelous physical phenomenon astonishes no one only so far as it puzzles the Embryologists. Why should our intellectual and inner growth, the evolution of the Human and Divine Spiritual, seem more impossible than the other?

The inner, now concealed man, was in the beginning the external man. His form then evolved from within outward, but after the cycle in which man began to procreate his species after the fashion of the present animal kingdom, it became the reverse. The human foetus follows now in its transformation all the forms that the physical frame of man assumed throughout the three Kalpas. In the present Age the physical embryo is a plant, a reptile, an animal before it finally becomes Man - evolving within himself his own ethereal counterpart.

At the end of three or four weeks in utero, the ovum has assumed a plant-like appearance, one extremity having become spherical and the other tapering like a carrot. If dissected at this time it is found to be composed like an onion of very delicate laminae or coats enclosing a liquid. These layers or coats approach each other at the lower end and the embryo hangs from the root of the umbilicus almost like the fruit from a bough; it is now a plant, and then the small creature begins to shoot out from the inside its limbs and develops the features; the eyes are visible as two black dots, the ears, nose and mouth form depressions. It looks like an animal the shape of a tadpole and like an amphibious reptile lives in water and develops from it. Its monad has not yet become human or immortal - this only occurs at the Fourth hour (Kabbalistic). One by one the foetus assumes the characteristics of the human being; the first flutter of immortal breath passes through its being, it moves and the Divine Essence settles in the infant frame.

As the foetus develops amidst the Liquor Amnii in the womb, so the Earth germinates in the Universal Ether or astral fluid in the womb of the Universe.

These cosmic children are first nucei, then ovules, then gradually mature, becoming mothers in their turn developing mineral, vegetable, animal, and human forms. From centre to circumference, from the imperceptible vesicle to the uttermost conceivable bounds of the Cosmos, great and glorious thinkers trace cycle merging into cycle containing and contained in an endless series, the Embryo evolving in its prenatal sphere - the individual in his family, the family in the state, the state in the mankind, the earth in our system, that system in its Central Universe, the Universe in the Kosmos and the Kosmos in the one cause, the Boundless and Endless.

And thus we discover the vast field for thorough expansion.

Concerning the rise and development of the functional activities of the embryo little is known of the various steps by which the primary fundamental qualities of the protoplasm of the ovum are differentiated into the complex phenomena of a perfect human body with various potencies of the one Unit unlike all others. The early history of humanity is not hidden; the little Ones of the earlier sub-races were entirely sexless and shapeless (no regular form) but those of the latter sub-races were born androgynous, and in the Third Race, separation of the Races began. Man bearing eggs commenced to give birth gradually and almost imperceptibly, first to beings in which one sex predominated over the other, then to distinct men and women; and the process of human foetal growth epitomizes the Third and Fourth Round of terrestrial life; and the potentiality of every organ useful to animal life is locked up in Man; at one period the human foetus has a tail twice the length of its nascent legs, and nowher is caution more to be advocated. Nowhere is premature judgment more to be deprecated than the attempt to bridge over the mysterious chasm which separates man from beast.

We are but beginning to understand something of the mighty records of the past. A century ago the world had not heard of Pompeii or Herculaneum, and knew nothing of the vast significance of the inscriptions upon the ancient tombs and temples of Egypt. Nothing of the meaning of the arrow-headed inscriptions of Babylon. Nothing of the great civilization revealed in the remains of Yucatan, Mexico and Peru, and we are now only on the threshold. Perhaps one hundred year from now the great Museums of the world may be adorned with gems and statues from submerged Atlantis, and the libraries containing translations of its in-

ons throw new light upon all the past history of the Human Races, solving
blems that now perplex the greatest thinkers of the Age.

"So mote it be."

-0-

THE SECOND RACE

By Dr. H. L. Henderson

eliminary. The Three first Races were Spirit, Soul and Body. The first
s Spirit, Motion, Life, etc. This Race had the Sense of Touch like a
g board, the word touch here would be quite the same as the feeling in
y, and as the Races evolved, this sense of touch differentiated into the
enses; in time must again become what he was during the Second Age, semi
al and Pure. The first human stock was projected by higher and Semi
Beings out of their own Essences.

tris and the Ancestors of the Adamic Races, which in the descending Evol-
receded our races of men, were the Spirits of human Races, or the Astral
adowed by Atma Buddhi falling into matter. The Puddingbags had Life and
ddhi but no Manas, and were therefore senseless. The reason for all evol-
s the gaining of experience; the best of us in the future will be Manasa
i.e., Mind Sons, or Sons of Mind finally identified with human Egos.
est of the human Life Wave will be the Pitris. Astral Body is first in
then comes the Germ that fructifies it. It is then clothed with Matter
the Pitris. The Chaaya is the lower mind, the shadow of the higher

e Continent prepared for the Second Race was named the Hyperborean; this
retched out its promontories Southward and Westward from the North Pole,
prised the whole of what is now known as Northern Asia. This far off
terious region was named by the Greeks, whither their tradition made
the Hyperborean travel every year. Apollo is the Sun, which in that far
untry is said never to set for one half of the year.

is land of the Hyperboreans, the country that extended beyond Boreas,
zen hearted God of snows, and hurricanes, who loved to slumber heavily
Chain of Mount Rhipaeus. It was neither an ideal country as surmised
Mythologists, nor yet a land in the vicinity of Scythia and the Danube;
was a real Continent, a bonafide Land which knew no winter in those
ays, nor has its sorry remains more than one night and day during the
w.

e Nocturnal Shadows never fall upon it (said the Greeks) <u>for it is the</u>
the Gods, the favorite abode of Apollo, the God of Light; such as the
the Second Race of Mankind.

This Second Race was produced by Budding and Expansion (get the analogy in the Second Month of the Embryonic Life in Utero). It was the A-sexual from the Sexless (i.e. - sex potency in Second Month). Thus O! Lanoo, was the Second Race produced. Their Fathers were the Self Born from the brilliant bodies of the Lords; the Sons of Twilight. The First Race was born under the Sun (i.e., Varuna God of the waters of Space or Akasa). The Second under Jupiter, God of Night (covering man's alienation unrelieved and unhindered).

At a banquet of Plato, Aristophanes speaks thus on the subject of antiquity. "Our nature of old was not the same as it is now; it was Androgynous, the form being common to both male and female; their bodies were round and the manner of running circular; revolving with the planet influence. They were terrible in force and strength and had prodigious ambition; hence Zeus (Ether) divided each of them into Two, making them weaker. Apollo, under his direction (obedient), closed up the skin. (Zeus - father of the Gods. Apollo - Sun God, or God of Light).

The Old Persians taught that man was the product of the Tree of Life, grow- ing in the androgynous pairs till they were separated by a subsequent modificatic of the human form. The correct Esoteric reading of Genesis would be as follows: The Elohim (i.e. - plural of God) brought forth from themselves (by modification) man: in Their Image created they him. (That is collective humanity, or Adam, male and female they (Collective Deity) created them; this will show the Eso- teric point. The Sexless Race was their first production; a modification of and from themselves, the pure Spiritual existence, and this was Adam Solus (i.e. - alone and solitary).

Thence came the Second Race, Adam Eve, or Jod Heva, inactive and androgyn- ous; then finally the Third or separating Hermaphrodite Cain and Abel; who pro- duced the Fourth, Seth Enes etc. The Third Race was the last Semi Spiritual; the last vehicle of Divine innate Wisdom. The Fourth tasted the Fruit of the Tree of Good and Evil, or impure intelligence; consequently they had to acquire that Wisdom by Intuition and great struggle; and the Union of Wisdom and Intel- ligence also. Wisdom ruling is called in the Hermetic Books, the God possessing the double fecundity of the two sexes; we find this symbolized in the Mythology of Zeus, a Male, but also an immortal Maid. The Egyptian Ammon was the Goddess Neith. Jupiter has female breasts, Venus is also represented with a beard; the name Adam implies this double form of existence; Thomas is rendered in Greek Didimos, a twin; and all the Gods of the primeval mankind were male and female. The Second Race was produced by budding and expansion, the Sexual form from the Sexless, or Shadow. This is a sexual Race, the most difficult to scientifically understand.

The Second, the fathers of the Sweat-born, so called, and perhaps still more the Third Race, the egg-born and androgynous; this Western mind can only with great difficulty understand these two modes of procreation, and no explan- ation can be attempted only to the Student of Occult Metaphysics. European language has no words to express things which Nature repeats no more at this stage of Evolution; (but there are analogies). It is not denied that at the beginning of physical evolution, there must have been a process in Nature now extinct; a spontaneous generation now repeated in other forms.

There is no difficulty in the conception of the primitive process of procreation; consider the first stage of the development of the Germ Cell. Its
development of nucleus as it grows changes and forms a double cone, or spindle;
this spindle approaches the surface of the cell, and one half of it is extruded
in the form of what are called the Polar Cells. These polar cells now die, and
the Embryo now develops from the growth and segmentation of the remaining part
of the nucleus which is nourished by the substance of the cell.

Then why could not Beings have been created and have lived in this way.
This may give you some idea by analogy, of the process by which the Second Race
was formed from the First. The Astral form clothing the Monad, was surrounded
- as it still is - by its Egg-shaped Sphere of Aura, which here corresponds to
the substance of the germ cell or Ovum. The Astral form is the nucleus now as
then, intuition with the Life Principle, when the Semen of reproduction arrives
the Sub-astral extrudes a miniature of itself from the egg of the surrounding
Aura; this germ grows and feeds on its surrounding aura until it becomes fully
developed, then it gradually separates from its parent carrying with it its own
sphere of aura, just as we see living cells reproducing their like by growth and
subsequent division into Two.

The analogy with the Polar Cell would seem to hold good, since there death
would now correspond to the change introduced by the separation of the Sexes,
when gestation in Utero within the cell became the rule. The early Second Root
Race were the fathers of the Sweat-born; then later the Second Root Race were
the Sweat-born themselves. The Sons of Yoga, or the Primitive Astral Race, had
Seven Stages of Racial Evolution as every individual being had, and has now.

The first Sub Race of the Second Race, were born at first by the process
described on the Law of Analogy; while the last began gradually with the Evolution of the human body to be formed otherwise. The process of reproduction
had seven stages also in each Race, each covering Aeons of time. What Scient-
ist can tell whether the present mode of generation, with all its phases of
Gestation, is older than half a million years, or at most one million. Since
their Cycle of observation began hardly half a century ago, who can tell?

Primeval Hermaphrodites of the human family were a fact in Nature, well
known to the Ancients; and form one of Darwin's greatest perplexities. Hermaph-
roditism existed in the evolution of the early races. By analogy and the Universal Law in Physical Evolution it must be so. A Talmudic axiom says: "If
thou wilt know the Invisible, open thine eyes to the Visible." It has long
been known that in the vertebral kingdom, one sex bears rudiments of various
accessory parts appertaining to the reproductive system which properly belonged
to the opposite sex. Some remote progenitor of the whole Vertebrate Kingdom
appears to have been Hermaphrodite or Androgynous; in the mammalian class, the
males possess rudiments of a Uterus with the adjacent passages in the vesienlae
prostatic; there are also rudiments of breasts, and some male marsupials have
traces of a marsupial sac. These relics of a prior Androgynous stock must be
placed in the same category as the Pineal Gland and other organs equally mysterious; which afford silent testimony as to the reality of functions now atro-
phied, but which once played a signal part in the general economy of primeval
life.

Details as to the submersion of the continent inhabited by the Second Race are not numerous; the submersion of Lemuria and Atlantis are given, but the others are only alluded to. The First Race is shown in Occult Science as Spiritual within and as Ethereal without. The Second as Psycho Spiritual mentally and Ethero-physical bodily. They were the Shadows of the Shadows of the Lords. These Shadows expanded; the spirits of the earth clothed them; the Solar Lhas (Sun Spirits) warmed them, i.e., preserved the Vital Fire in the nascent physical forms. The breath had Life but no Understanding, they had no fire or water of their own. This Fire is the Higher Self, the Spiritual Ego; that which propells toward and forces evolution.

The higher spiritual Nature on this plane, being in bondage to the lower, the First Race created the Second by budding; the Second gives birth to the Third, which is separated into Three distinct divisions consisting of men differently procreated; the first two of these produced by an Oviperous method (producing eggs) unknown to natural history; while the early sub-races of the third humanity, procreated their species by a kind of exudation of moisture, or a vital fluid, the drops of which coalescing formed an egg-shaped ball that served as an extraneous vehicle for the generation therein of a Foetus and child. Later the mode of procreation changed.

The little ones of the early sub-races were entirely sexless and for all that we know shapeless; but later they were born androgynous; from being first a sexless humanity, they became distinctly Hermaphrodite or bi-sexual; and finally a man bearing eggs, began to give birth, gradually and almost imperceptibly in their evolutionary development, first to beings in which one sex predominated over the other, and finally to distinct Men and Women.

In analogy to the egg-born, bear in mind that in one sense Humanity is now egg-born; the Uterus assuming that shape during gestation. Now the point insisted upon at present is that whatever origin be claimed for man, his evolution took place in this order; First - Sexless, as all the earlier forms are. Second - by a natural transition, he then became a Solitary Hermaphrodite, a bisexual being, and Third - he separated and finally became what he now is. Bi-sexual Reproduction is an evolution, a specialized and perfected procreated form on the scale of matter.

The Fissiparous (i.e., split separated bring forth) act of reproduction, is the bi-sexual. Occult teachings are preeminently Panspermic (i.e., all objects must come from living parents, biogenesis etc.) and the early history of humanity is hidden from ordinary mortals, (which includes most of the populace).

From the First Race emanated the Second, called the Sweat-born and the boneless; it was endowed by the preservers and the incarnating Gods with the first primitive and weak spark (or germ) of intelligence; and from these came the third Root Race, the two-fold androgynous. The first races thereof are Shells till the last is inhabited (i.e., informed) by the Dhyanis. The Second Race, Sexless, evolved out of itself, at its beginning, the third Androgynous Race by an analogous but already more complicated process the Sons of Passive Yoga; they issued from the Second human race and became Oviparous; the emanations that came out of their bodies during the seasons of procreation, were ovulary; this small spherical nuclei developed into a large soft egg-like vehicle which gradually hardened, then after a period of gestation it broke and the young animal issued from it unaided as the fowls in our races.

The analogy here is the Ovule; after impregnation, Foetal development takes place as in the egg; the Primitive Race merged into the Second Race and became one with it; this race never died, it just gradually melted away; becoming absorbed into the bodies of their own sweat-born progeny. When the Astral body became covered with more solid flesh, man developed a physical body; and this is the meaning of the Greek Myth of Leda and her two Sons Castor and Pollox. Jupiter endows them with a marvelous gift and privilege; they are Semi-Immortal. The Hindu allegory of Marisha is a symbol of the Second Race of Mankind; and the Mexican Legends that tell of the primitive ancestors who could act and live with equal ease under ground and water as upon the earth, refers to the Second and early Third Race.

The Old Commentary says: Universal Genesis starts from the One, breaks into three, then five, and finally culminates in the seven, to return to four, three and one. The Sons of Mahat (i.e., the first principle of Universal Intelligence and Consciousness) are the quickeners of the Human Plant; they are the waters falling upon the arid soil of latent Life and the spark that vivifies the human animal. They are the Lords of Spiritual Life Eternal.

In the Second Race some of these Lords only breathed of their essence into Man; and some took up in Man their abode. This race had a sound language; Chant -like sounds composed of vowels alone; just an open position of the mouth organs of speech structures. The Allegories of this Second or Sweat-born Race, concealed a psycho-physiological phenomenon, and one of the greatest mysteries of Nature; (i.e., feminine power) Sweat exudations of moisture. Eros was connected in early Greek Mythology with the World's Creation, and later became the Sexual Cupid.

Such was the Karma in his original Vedic Character; the allegory shows the Psychic element developing the physiological. Before the birth of Daksha (i.e., the progenitors of real physical man) who was born from Marshia, and before whose time, living beings and men were procreated by the Will, by Sight, by Touch and by Yoga. The very early Third Races was formed from the drops of sweat, which after many transformations, grew into human bodies. This is not more difficult to imagine or realize than the growth of the Foetus from an imperceptive Germ, and its subsequent development into a child, and then into a strong heavy Man. Huge eggs were produced in this race, in which later the Human Foetus gestated for several years. (40).

This explains why Aristophanes, in Plato's Banquet, describes the nature of the old race as androgynous. The form of every individual being rounded; having its back and sides as in a Circle; whose manner of running was Circular. They were terrible in strength and force and with prodigious ambition; so therefore to weaken them, Zeus (Father of Ether) divided them into two.

The Madagascar Island belonged to Lemuria, and the natives there have a tradition about the first man; that he lived without eating, and having indulged in food, a swelling appeared in his leg; this bursting there emerged from it a female who became the Mother of their Race. The sexual Lemurians evolved from Hermaphrodite Parents, quite unlike its immediate progenitors; and it is unquestionable that in human incarnations, the law of Karma, Racial or Individual, overrides the subordinate tendencies of Heredity, its servant.

In recapitulation we read as follows - The Second Race evolved the Egg-born (i.e., the third). The sweat grew, its drops grew, and the drops became hard and round (sweat exudations), the Sun warmed it, the Moon cooled and shaped it, the Wind fed it until its ripeness. The White Swan (i.e. Moon), overshadowed the big drop; the egg of the future races from the Starry Vault (Moon). The Man Swan (i.e., Hamsa, a mysterious Bird in Occultism) is analogous to the Rosicrucian Pelican. This Bird, out of space and time, said to descend into the universe for purposes of manifestation, of the later Third Race, first male-female, then man and woman. This text implies that the human Embryo was nourished (abestra), by methods of external or Cosmic Forces; and that the Father-Mother furnished apparently, the Germ that ripened, to be hatched out in some mysterious way, disconnected from the double Parent. Right Wing, -U it's Left, and M its Tail; and the Ardha Matra (half Metre and Rhythm) was In its head. A Yoga who bestrides the Hamsa (Man Swan), meaning that he contemplates upon A-U-M, is not affected by Karmic influences or Crores (i.e., millions of Sins).

The third Race is sometimes called collectively, the Sons of Passive Yoga; this was produced unconsciously by the Second Race which as it was intellectually inactive, is supposed to have been constantly plunged in a kind of blank or abstract contemplation, as was required by the conditions of the Yoga state (this is the deep sleep of Adam).

The Third Race in its early existence was produced by Kriyashakti; a progeny called the Sons of Ad, or the Fire Mist, the Sons of Will and Yoga; they were a conscious production, as a portion of the Race and already animated with the Divine Spark of superior Spiritual Intelligence. This progeny was not a Race, it was a wonderful Being, and after it a group of Semi-Divine and semi-human beings were set apart in Archaic Genesis for certain purposes to form the Nursery for future human Adepts on this Earth. And during the present Cycle, these Sons of Will and Yoga, born so to speak in an immaculate way, remained entirely apart from the rest of mankind; and the Secret Doctrine tells they remain at their post until the last day of this life Cycle; for the lonely sore footed pilgrims on their journey back to their home, are never sure to the last moment, of not losing their way in this limitless desert of illusion, called matter and earth life. He would fain show the way to that region of freedom and Light (from which he is a voluntary exile) to every prisoner who has succeeded in liberating himself from the bonds of flesh and illusion.

Uranus is said to be one of the Seven Dhyan Chohans; and the first Astronomical Teacher of the Second Race; Thus the Chinese revere Tien, or Ouranos. Uranus gave birth to the Titans of the Third Race personified by Saturn Cronus who mutilated him, for they fell into generation; when Creation by Will was superceded by physical procreation they needed Uranus no more. The Celestial Group of Uranus ruled over the Second Race and their then Hyperborean Continent. The name Hypoborean signifies beyond Boreas, or the North Wind; presumably the same as the Sacred Land.

In the Vendidad, Yima is called the first man, his twin brother Yama the Son of Vaivasrata Maun belongs to the two Epochs of Universal History, representing the First and Second Races. They were the Spiritual Progenitors of Mankind. These Races never died, they dissolved, disappearing in their progeny; and the Third knew death only toward the close. After the Separation of the Sexes, Yima refuses to become the bearer of the Law of Ahura Mazda, saying, " I was not taught to be the Preacher or bearer of Thy Law." Then Ahura asks him to increase men and watch over his world. He says yes I will nourish and rule and watch over Thy World; there shall be, while I am King neither Cold or Hot Wind (vibration) neither disease nor death. Then Ahura Mazda b ings him a golden ring and poinard, the emblems of Sovereignty. Under this sway of Yima, three hundred Cycles passed away; and the earth was replenished with flocks and herds, with men, dogs and birds, and red blazing fires. Mark well the word replenished, it means filled again; that is to say this had been on it before.

Thus is proven the knowledge of successive destructions of the World and its Life Cycles. Once the three hundred Cycles pass away, Ahura warns Yima that the Earth is becoming too full and men have no where to live. Then Yima steps forward, and with the help of Spenta Armaita, the Female Genius, or Spirit of the Earth, causes the Earth to increase in size. Nine Hundred Cycles pass away and Yima has to perform the same ceremony for the Third Time.

This Allegory is the Old Mazdean or Persian symbolism for the Flood. Ahura warning Yima in an assembly of Celestial Gods and excellent Mortals, that fatal Winters will fail, and all life perish. This was the destruction of Atlantis which swept away all Races in turn. Yima makes an enclosure, an ark, and under the direction of God, brings thither the seed of every living creature animal and fires. This was the beginning of the Fourth Race after the men of the Third began to die out; till then there had been no regular death, only transformation, for man had no personality; they had impersonal monads and shadow bodies; Sinless, hence Karmaless. Therefore there was no Karma, no Kama Loka, no Nirvana, no Devachan; for the sons of men, who had no personal Egos there could be no intermediate periods between Incarnations. Like the Phoenix, primordial Man resurrected out of his old body, into the new body each time, and with each new generation, he became more solid, more physically perfect.

Agreeably with the Evolution Law, which is the Law of Nature, Death came with the complete physical organism, and with it Moral decay. Mankind did not issue from one solitary couple, nor was there people called man, Adam, or Yiva, but a first Mankind, and that which people called the Highest God, is not a substance, but the cause of it. Not one that is here, there or elsewhere, nor what we see, but that in quest of Light.

Teach us, O God, how to learn Thy Wisdom. Divine Reason Alone can aid this Storm Tossed World.

In this Race we find our analogy in the Third Month of Life in Utero where distinct sex manifests. The Second Race evolved the Egg Born or Third Race; the Egg of the Future Race, the Man Swan of the later Third, first male-female then Man and Woman. The worship of the Third Race was the most ancient of all the Hermaphrodites, in which the Male Moon became sacred, when after the so-called Fall the sexes became separated the Deus Lunus (Moon God) then became an androgyne Male and Female in turn to finally serve for purposes of sorcery as a dual power of the Fourth Root Race, the Atlanteans. The dual aspect of the Moon, the worship of the female and male principles respectively ended in distinct Solar and Lunar Cults among the Semetic Races. The Sun was for a long time feminine and the Moon masculine, the latter idea being adapted by them from the Atlantean traditions. In the infancy of the third Race a creature of a more exalted kind was yet wanting, and therefore was designed conscious of thought, of more capacious breast for Empire formed and fit to Rule. A perfect vehicle was called into being for the incarnating denizens of higher spheres, they took their abodes in these forms born of Spiritual Will and the Natural Divine power (Kriyashakti) in Man. It was a Child of pure Spirit, mentally un-alloyed with any tincture of Earthly elements. Its physical frame alone was of time and of life, for it drew its intelligence from above. He was the First of the First and the seed of all the others; there were other Sons of Kriya-sakti produced by the second spiritual effort, but the first one has remained to this day the seed of Divine Knowledge (Planetary Spirit). The Third Race is sometimes called collectively the Sons of passive Yoga. It was produced un-consciously by the Second Race which, as it was intellectually inactive, is supposed to have been constantly plunged in a kind of blank or abstract con-templation as required by the conditions of the Yoga state (the deep sleep of Adam).

In the beginning of this Third Race while it was yet in its state of pur-ity, the Sons of Wisdom incarnated and produced by Kriyashakti a progeny cal-led the Sons of Ad, or the Fire Mist - the Sons of Will and Yoga; they were a conscious production, as a portion of the Race was already animated with the Divine Spark of Spiritual Superior Intelligence. This progeny was not a Race but a wondrous Being descended from a higher region; this was before the separ-ation of the sexes. In the early part of the Third Race after this came a group of Semi-Divine and semi-human Beings set apart in archaic genesis for certain purposes, (not all separated in the same way) and under the direct sil-ent guidance of this wonderful Being all the other less Divine Teachers and Instructors of mankind became from the first awakening of human consciousness the guides of early humanity.

It is through these Sons of God that Infant humanity learned its first notions of all the Arts and Sciences, as well as spiritual knowledge, and it is they who laid the first foundation stone of ancient civilization that have so puzzled our modern generation of students and scholars. Such works did not develop from lower animal-like savages, the cave-men etc. No man thus develop-ed could ever evolve such a science unaided even in millenniums of thought and intellectual evolution.

It is the pupils of these incarnated Rishis and Devas of the Third Root Race who handed on their knowledge from one generation to another. To Egypt and to Greece, with her long lost canon (i.e., Rule) of the proportions and just so the Atlanteans passed it over to their Cyclops Sons of Cycles; they

-15-

passed it on to the still later generations of Gnostic Priests. And it is owing to the Divine perfection of those architectural proportions that the student could build these wonders of all subsequent Ages, Fanes, Pyramids, cave-temples, Cromlechs, Cairns, etc., proving that they had the power of machinery and the knowledge of mechanics to which modern skill is like child's play. They used neither mortar nor cement, nor steel or iron to cut their stones with, and yet they were so artfully wrought that in many places the joints were hardly seen. There are stones in the Peruvian buildings 38 feet long, 18 feet broad and 6 feet thick; and in Cuzco and other places there are stones beautifully cut of greater size. The well of Syene (i.e., Assoane), made over 5,000 years ago, when that spot was exactly under the propic, was so constructed that at noon, at the precise moment of the Solar Solstice the entire disc of the Sun was seen reflected in its surface - a work which the united skill of all the architects and astronomers in Europe would not now be able to effect.

These spiritually descended Sons of Will and Yoga became in time divided into opposite sexes as their Kriyasakti progenitors did themselves later on. Yet even their degenerate descendants have, down to the present day, retained a veneration and respect for the creative functions and still regard them in the light of a religious ceremony. Whereas the more civilized nations (so called Christians) consider it as a mere animal function. Compare the Western views and practices in these matters with the Institutions of Manu. He whose seven forefathers have drunk the juice of the Moon Plant (Soma), understanding the secret of the Vedas; to this day such Brahmans know that during the early beginning of the Race psychic and physical intellect being dormant, and consciousness still undeveloped. Its spiritual conceptions were quite undeveloped, unconnected with time its physical surroundings.

Divine man dwelt in his animal, though externally human form; if there was instinct in him no self-consciousness came to enlighten the darkness of the latent fifth principle. When the Lords of Wisdom moved by the Law of Evolution infused into him the spark of consciousness, the very first feeling it awoke to life and activity was a sense of solidarity of oneness with his spiritual creators, as the childs first feeling is for its mother and nurse, so the first aspirations of the awakening consciousness in primitive man, were for those whose elements he felt within himself, and who were yet outside and independent of him. Devotion arose out of that feeling and became the first and foremost motor in his nature; it is natural and innate in his heart and we find it in the human babe and the young of animal; the essence of it lives through all time and eternity, and has settled in all its ineradicable strength and power in the Asiatic Aryan heart.

From the third Race direct through its first mind-born Sons, the fruits of Kriyasakti, the Third Race became the Vahan of the Lords of Wisdom; at the dawn of his consciousness the man of the Third Root Race had no beliefs that could be called Religion. He was ignorant of any religion, full of pomp and gold and void of any system of faith or outward worship, but there was a binding to gether of the masses in one form of reverence paid to those we feel higher than ourselves. That made the Lemurian Religion beautiful. From the beginning of their intellectual life they had no bright Gods of the Elements around and within themselves and their childhood was passed with those who had given them being and called them forth to intelligent consciousness of life. It was the

Golden Age when the Gods walked the Earth and mixed freely with the mortals. But the abuses of the creative power has changed mankind from a healthy King of animals creation in the Third Race to the helpless scrofulous being of our Fifth Race until he has now become the wealthiest heir on the globe to constitutional disease as well as that of heredity and the most intelligently bestial of all animals.

That Third and Holy Race consisted of men who, at their zenith, were described as towering giants of Godly strength and beauty, and the depositories of all the mysteries of Heaven and Earth. When the Sweat-born produced the Egg-born, the two fold androgyne Third Race, the mighty and powerful with bones, the Lords of Wisdom said: "Now shall we create." The Third Race became then the vehicle of the Lords of Wisdom. It created Sons of Will and Yoga by Kriyashakti, that mysterious power of thought which enables it to produce external perceptible phenomenal results by its own inherent energy. An idea will manifest externally if our attention and will are deeply concentrated upon it. This same power by which they first created, is that which has since caused them to be degraded from their high status to the position of evil spirits of Satan and his host. Kriyashakti is that mysterious and Divine power latent in all the will of every man which, if not called to life, quickened and developed by Yoga training remains dormant in 999,999 out of every million, and so atrophies. The Third Race had thus created the ancestors, the Spiritual Forefathers, in a truly immaculate way. They were indeed created and not begotten, for creation is but the result of Will acting on phenomenal Matter, the calling forth out of the Primordial Divine Light and eternal matter, the calling forth out of the Primordial Divine Light and eternal Life. They were the "Holy Seed Grain" of the Future Saviours of Humanity.

The Third Race, the Sweat-born, the Egg-born and Androgynous were almost sexless in its early beginnings. It became bisexual or androgynous very gradually of course; passing from the first to the last transformation, required numberless generations, during which the simple cell that issued from the earliest parents (the two in one), developed first into a bisexual being and then the cell became a regular Egg gave forth a unisexual creature.

The Third Race mankind is the most mysterious of all the developed Races; the mystery of the how, of the generation of the distinct sexes and a specialist, only a faint outline of the process is possible. But it is evident that the Units of the Third Race Humanity began to separate in their prenatal shells or eggs and to issue out of them as distinct Male and Female Babes. Ages after the appearance of its early progenitors toward the end of the Fourth Sub Race of the Third Race, the Babe lost its faculty of walking as soon as liberated from its shell, and by the end of the Fifth Sub Race, mankind was born under the same conditions and by the same process as our historical generation. Babes at birth being the most helpless creatures; this required millions of years.

The Second Race had a sound language, chant-like, composed of vowels alone. The Third Race, in the beginning, developed a kind of language which was only a slight improvement on the various sounds in Nature. The cry of gigantic insects and the first animals. In its second half the Sweat-born gave birth to the Egg-born, the middle Third Race, and when these, instead of hatching out

as androgynous beings to evolve into the separate male and females, and when
the same law of evolution led them to reproduce their kind sexually, an act
which forced the Creative Gods, compelled by Karmic Law, to incarnate in mindless men, then only was speech developed, but it was only an experiment; and
all humanity at this time had but one language; however this did not prevent
the last two sub-races from building Cities and sowing far and wide the first
seed of civilization under the guidance of their Divine Instructors and their
own already awakened mind.

At the close of the Third Root Race the Yellow Colored, after their separation into sexes and the full awakening of their mind, they had a monosyl-
labic speech; before that they communicated by what is now called thought
transference; though outside of the Sons of Wisdom thought was but little
developed, and never soared above a low terrestrial level; their physical bodies belonged to the Earth, their Monads remained on a higher plane altogether.
Language could not be developed before the acquisition of reasoning faculties.

The Third Race built boats and flotillas before it built houses. The animals separated first into male and female; they then began to breed. The two-
fold man then separated also, and said let us, as they, unite and make creatures. They did, and those which had no Spark, the narrow headed, took she
animals unto them. They were dumb and begat Dumb-Races but their tongues un-
tied, the tongues of their progeny remained still, Monsters they bred. A race
of crooked re-hair-covered monsters going on all fours. A dumb race to keep
the shame untold. These monsters are not the Anthropoid, or any other Apes,
but what the Anthropologist might call the missing link; the primitive lower
man.

The animals separated first. Bear in mind that men were different even
physically from what they are now, and the huge she animals were different
from any we now know. This was the first fall into matter, the first Physical fall of some of the then existing and lower Races.

The Sons of Wisdom had spurned the early Third Race, the non-developed,
and are shown incarnating in, and thereby endowing with Intellect, the latter
Third Race. Thus the sin of the mindless who had no spark and were irresponsible, fell upon those who failed to do their Karmic duty by them.

Occultism rejects the idea that Nature developed Man from the Ape or even
from the ancestor common to both.

Use and disuse, combined with selection, elucidates the separation of the
sexes, and the instance (otherwise totally incomprehensible) of rudimentary
sexual organs in the vertebrate especially. Each sex possesses such distinct
traces of the reproductive apparatus characteristic of the other, that even
antiquity assumed Hermaphrodittsus as a natural primitive state or condition of
mankind.

The mysteries of Heaven and Earth revealed to the Third Race by their Celestial Teachers in the days of their purity, became a great focus of Light, the
rays from which became necessarily weakened as they were diffused and shed upon
an uncongenial, because too material shape of exoteric Religions of idolatry

full of superstition, and man or hero worship. Alone a handful of primitive men remained the elect custodians of the mysteries revealed to mankind by the Divine Teachers. They saw the Divine Wisdom grow dim in those who turned it to evil purposes, and with more intensity, kept the spark burning within themselves. There were those among them who remained in their Kumaric State (i.e., Virgin Youth) condition from the beginning, and tradition whispers that these elect were the Germ of a Hierarchy, which has never died since that period.

The Inner School says that out of the Seven Virgin Men (Kumara) four sacrificed themselves for the Sins of the World, and for the <u>instruction of the</u> ignorant to remain till t-e end of the present Manvantara. Though unseen they are ever present; when people say of them "He is dead", behold he is alive and under another form. These Four are the Head, the Heart, the Soul and the Seed of Undying Knowledge. "Thou shalt never speak 'O Lanoo' of these Great Ones before a multitude mentioning their names." The wise alone will <u>understand.</u>

The Continent of Lemuria which served as the cradle of the Great Third Race, not only embraced a vast area in the Pacific and Indian Oceans, but extended in the shape of a horse-shoe past Madagascar, around South Africa (then a mere fragment in process of formation), through the Atlantic up to Norway. Here at the Arctic Circle (Norway) the Lemurian Continent began to sink, and the Third Race ended its career in Lanka, the small remnant now known as Ceylon in the Northern Highland of Ancient Lanka, that enormous Island of the Lemurian Period. But bear in mind that continuity in natural processes is never broken, and Greek, Roman, and even Egyptian civilizations are nothing compared to the civilization <u>that began</u> with the Third Race, <u>after</u> its separation.

Easter Island belongs to the earliest civilization of the Third Race. It was a volcanic and sudden uplifting of the Ocean Floor which raised this small relic of the Archaic Ages after it had been submerged with the rest; untouched with its volcano and statues, as a standing witness to the existence of Lemuria, a gigantic continent, which during the Third Race stretched East and West, as far as where the two Americas now lie. The present Australia was but a portion of it, and in addition there are a few surviving Islands strewn hither and thither on the face of the Pacific, and a large strip of California belonged to it; and in some of the flat-headed Aborigines of Australia behold the relics of that once great Nation, now so nearly extinct.

About the middle part of the development of the Third Race, the axel of the Wheel Tilted. The Sun and Moon shone no longer over that portion of the heads of the Sweat-born; the people knew snow, ice and frost; and men, plants and animals were dwarfed in their growth, and after the great flood of the Third Race, men decreased <u>considerably in stature</u>; and the duration of their lives was diminished.

Having fallen down in Godliness, they mixed with animal races and intermarried among giants and pigmies (i.e., dwarfed races of the Poles). Man acquired Divine, nay more - unlawful Knowledge, and willingly followed the Left-hand Path.

Plato knew about the history of the Third Race after its fall, but he never spoke of it, for he was pledged to secrecy. The Third Race fell and Created no longer, - it Begat; its progeny still mindless at the period of separation. It begat, moreover, anomalous offspring until its physiological nature had adjusted its instincts in the right direction.

The Dhyan Chohans had warned it to leave alone the fruit forbidden by Nature; but the warning proved of no value. Men realized the unfitness of what they had done only when too late. When the physical triumphed over the spiritual and mental evolution, and nearly destroyed it, the great gift of the Kriyashakti remained, the heirloom of only a few elect men in every Age. Spirit strove vainly to manifest itself in its fullness, in purely organic forms; and the faculty which had been a natural attribute in the early humanity of the Third Race, came to be regarded as phenomenal by Spiritualists and Occultists, and as scientifically impossible by materialists.

Only after the so-called fall, did the Races begin to develop rapidly into a purely human shape. The torpor of the first half of the Third Race, is symbolized by the deep sleep of Adam, mentioned in the Second Chapter of Genesis; it is the dreamless sleep of mental inaction, the slumber of the Soul and Mind. When spirituality and all the Divine Powers and Attributes of the Deva Man of the Third Race had been made the handmaidens of the newly awakened physiological and psychic passions of the physical, instead of the reverse, the Third Eye lost its powers. But such was the Law and it was in strict accuracy no Fall. The Sin was not in using these newly developed powers, but in misusing them; in making of the Tabernacle designed to contain a God, the fane of every Spiritual iniquity (i.e., made of this Tabernacle a Tavern); there can be no physical iniquity, for the body is simply the irresponsible organ, the tool of the psychic, if not of the spiritual man.

Seth in the Bible represents the later Third Race. The Sons of God have existed and do exist. There were Giants in the Earth before the sinless Sons of the Third Race, and also after that when other Sons of God lower in nature, inaugurated sexual connection on Earth.

Creative powers in man were the gift of Divine Wisdom; not the result of sin, nor was the curse of Karma called down upon them for seeking natural union, as all the mindless animal world does in its proper season, but for Abusing the Creative Power, for desecrating the Divine Gift, and wasting the Life Essence for no purpose, except bestial personal gratification.

In the beginning, Generation was as easy for Woman as it was for all animal creation. Nature had never intended that woman should bring forth her young in sorrow. The suffering was brought about by turning the Holy Mystery of procreation into animal gratification. And Intellectual Evolution in its progress, hand in hand with the physical, has certainly been a curse instead of a blessing. Disease and over-population are facts which cannot be denied.

The Sons of Will and Yoga of the Third Race were indeed Created, not Begotten, for creation is but the result of Will, acting on Phenomenal Matter; the calling forth out of it, of the Primordial Divine Light and Eternal Life. The Third and Holy Race consisted of men who, at their zenith were described as towering Giants of Heaven and Earth; and the Chief Gods and Heroes of the Fourth and Fifth Races are the defiled images of these men of the Third. This Race could live with equal ease in water, air or fire, for it had an unlimited control over the Elements.

These were the Sons of God, and it was they who imparted Nature's most weird secrets to men, and revealed to them, the Ineffable, and now lost word.

Castor and Pollux symbolize the Third Race and its transformation from the animal man, into the God Man, with only an animal body - Sphinx. Three Yugas (the 1,000th part of a Kalpa E.G.) are said to have passed away during the time of the Third Root Race, the Satua, the Treta and Drapara (i.e., the Golden Age) in its early innocence, the Silver when it reached its maturity, and the Bronze Age when separating into Sexes.

The Mind Born, the boneless, gave birth to the Will Born with bones. This took place 18,000,000 years ago; about the middle of the Third Race, and the antiquity of the First Race dates back millions of years beyond this again; we are told the exact figures are withheld, but one thing is clear - that the 18,000,000 years embrace the duration of sexual physical Man, must be enormously increased if the whole process of Spiritual, Astral, and Physical development is taken into account.

We are asked how could primordial man exist in the dense agglomeration of vapors charged with Carbonic Acid Gas that escaped from the soil, or was held in suspension in the atmosphere; in reply we know that such terrestrial conditions were then operative but they had no touch with the Planes on which the evolution of the Etherial Astral Races proceeded. In these early ages, Astral evolution was in progress only, and the two Planes, the astral and the physical had no direct point of contact with one another, although developing on parallel lines; and we must understand, that this Earth did not reach its present grade of Density until about 18,000,000. Since then both the physical and astral planes have become grosser.

Life has not always reigned on this Terrestrial Plane. There was a time when the simple Globule of Protoplasm, had not yet appeared at the bottom of the seas, whence came the impulse producing Carbon, Nitrogen, Osygen Protoplasm etc.

Your Earth got its supply of Life Germs from other Planets; Who, or What carried them on to these Planets? Here again we must accept occult teaching or face a Miracle?

Active Creators are known to exist; they are sensed by the Inner Man, and Divine Thought pervades these numberless active Creating Forces of Creators. They are moved by, and have their being from and through Divine Thought, which however has no personal concern in them or their Creations; no more than the Sun has for the flower and its seeds.

Nature is a habit moved from itself, according to seminal principles. The conditions that were necessary for the Earliest Race of Mankind, required no Elements, simple or compound.

-21-

Spiritual and Etherial Entities live in Spaces unknown to Earth, before the first Siderial Jelly Speck evolved in the Ocean of crude Cosmic Matter, billions and billions of years before our Globe Earth came into existence. And Manu with soft bones, could well dispense with Calcium Phosphate - he had no bones to require it; and the primitive ancestors of our Legends, who could act and live with equal ease under ground or water, as upon the Earth, refers only to the Second and Third Early Races.

The Universal Genesis starts from One, breaks into Three, then Five, and finally culminates in Seven; to return to Four, Three and back to One. Thus we learn the Majesty and Vastness of Nature revealing to us in earnest study, the Great Highway from Protoplasm back to God or Divine Thought.

FOURTH RACE

Two by two on the Seven Zones the Third Race gave birth to the Fourth. The first on every Zone was Moon colored, the Second Yellow like Gold, the Third Red, the Fourth Brown, which became black with sin. The first seven human shoots were all of one complexion; the next seven began mixing, then the Third and Fourth became tall with pride. They took wives from the mindless. They bred wicked Demons. They built Temples for the human body. Male and Female they worshipped them. The Third Eye acted no longer. They built huge cities of rare earths and metals. They built out of fires vomited out of the white stones of the mountains and of the black stone (lava). They cut their own Images nine Jatis high the size of their bodies (a Jati equals three feet of our measure) this equals 27 feet, the height of the Lemuria-Atlantean bodies. Inner fires had destroyed the land of their fathers, the Water threatened the Fourth. The men who preceded the Atlantean Race, however much they may have looked physically like the gigantic Ape, were still a thinking, and already speaking man. The Lemuro Atlantean was a highly civilized Race, and if one accepts tradition which is better history than the speculative fiction which now passes under that name, he was farther advanced at the closing of the Third Race than we are with all our sciences and degraded civilization of the present time.

The Gods of primeval mankind were male and female, but modern mind is satisfied to worship the Male Heroes of the Fourth Race who created Gods after their own image.

Adam or Man, applies to a double form of existence. Adam Solus was the first life upon the planet. The second was Adam Eve, or Jod Heva, inactive, androgynous. Then the Third, Cain and Abel, or the active separating Hermaphrodites from which sprung the Fourth Race, Seth Enos etc. The third was the last semi-spiritual, the last vehicle of the Innate Wisdom ingenerated in the

-22-

Enochs, the Seers of that mankind. The Fourth had tasted of the Fruit of the Tree of Good and Evil, or early wisdom, therefore impure intelligence, and had consequently to acquire that Divine Wisdom by Initiation and great struggle. And this wisdom uniting and ruling intelligence is called in the Hermetic Books, the God possessing the double fedundity of the two sexes. The two important twin births of Genesis, that of Cain and Abel, Esau and Jacob show the same idea.

Abel or Hevel, is the same as Eve.

Creative powers in humanity were the gift of Divine Wisdom, not the result of Sin. The Curse was not brought on mankind by the Fourth Race, for the Third Race had perished in the same way. The deluge was no punishment, but simply a result of periodical and geological Law, nor was the curse of Karma called down upon them for seeking natural union, as all the mindless animal world does in its proper season, but for abusing the Creative Power, for desecrating the Divine Gift and wasting the Life Essence for no purpose except a bestial personal gratification.

The third Chapter of Genesis refers to the Adam and Eve of the Closing Third, and the commencing Fourth Races, where we learn that natural Law never intended that Woman should bring forth her young in sorrow, for in the beginning gestation and birth was easy. But during the evolution of the Fourth Race, there came enmity between its fructifying power and the Seed, or product of Karma and Divine Wisdom.

Then the Holy Mystery of procreation was changed into animal gratification, and the whole nature of the Fourth Race of mankind was changed physiologically, morally, physically and mentally; and from being the healthy King of animals, created in the Third Race, Man has become in our present Race a helpless, scrofulous being, the wealthiest heir on the globe to constitutional and hereditary diseases, the most consciously and intelligently bestial of all animals.

Viewed from this aspect, the curse is undeniable, for it is evident that the intellectual evolution in its progress, hand in hand with its physical, has certainly been a curse instead of a blessing.

Disease and over-population are facts that can never be denied. The evolution of the Fourth Race led down to the very bottom of materiality in its physical development, but this present Race is on the ascending arc, and the Race to follow this will rapidly grow out of the bonds of matter.

It is from the Fourth Race that the early Aryans got their knowledge of wonderful things; from them they learned Aeronatuics called Vimana, Viduya, or the knowledge of flying air vehicles. And also from them came the most valuable Sciences, Chemistry, Geology, Minerology, Physics, Astronomy etc. It is said that one of the Kings of the Divine Dynasty, imparted to the Fourth Race the symbol of Venus, which is a circle over the cross; and the Earth a circle under the cross (or a cross within the Circle) meaning the Earth had fallen into generation, or the production of the species as at the present time.

Venus is the most Occult, powerful and mysterious of all the Planets. Its

-23-

relation to and influence upon our Earth is most prominent, it is Hermaphro-
ditic, hence the bearded Venus in Mythology, and through its influence the
double ones of the Third Root Race descended from the First Sweat Born.

The Fourth Race Atlanteans were developed from a nucleus, of North Lemurian Third Race men, centered toward a point of land in what is now the mid-
Atlantic Ocean. Their continent was formed by the coalescence of many islands
and peninsulas which were upheaved, and ultimately became the true home of the
Fourth Race.

There are great cycles of the fall and rise of Nations and Races, and when
those of the Fourth mixed with the giants of the land of iniquity, they became
black with sin, and lost the wealth and glory of A. U. M. From the third Race
was the Fourth born, and that portion of humanity which had become black with
sin, was gradually transformed into Red-Yellow (the Red Indians and Mongolians
being their present descendents) and finally into Brown-White Races, which now
together with the Yellow Races, form the great bulk of humanity.

Until the beginning of the Fourth Race, when the Third began to die out,
there was no regular death; but only a transformation; for mankind had no personality as yet. Their shadow bodies were Karma-less, there was no Kama Loka,
no Devachan or Nirvana, for the Souls who had no personal Egos there could be
no intermediate periods between incarnations. Like the Phoenix primordial mankind resurrected out of the old into a new body, each time he became more physically perfect, more solid, agreeable with evolutionary Law, which is the Law
of Nature.

Death came with the complete physical organism and with it moral decay.
But the Fourth Race had its period of the highest civilization to which the
Greek, Roman, and even Egyptian did not compare. And this civilization began
with the Third Race after its separation; but if this is denied, no one can
deny that between this great civilization of Egypt and India there was stretched,
dark ages of crass ignorance and barberism, and ever since the Constantine era
of Christianity up to our own so-called civilization, all recollection of these
valuable traditions have been lost, and the thinking people of today know that
future generations will turn their page of history back to this present time of
darkness; this so-called Christian Era, and read of the most soulless and in-
human selfishness, midst a semi-barberous environment of ignorance, duplicity,
egoism, cruelty and crime, that ever disgraced and degraded any Race of Human
Life upon our dark and sorrowful Planet.

It is a question of how long the Great Universal protecting forces will
sustain a world that brings forth such a maximum of evil. In the Eocene, or
first Geological subdivision of the great Cycle of the Fourth Race, Men. had
already reached its highest point of civilization; and their great Continent,
the Parent of nearly all present Continents, showed the first symptoms of sinking; and Atlantis as a whole perished during the Miocene, or middle Geological
division. The last Island of Atlantis went down about 11,000 years ago. The
great deluge carried away the remaining Atlantean people, and changed the
whole face of the Earth.

The mighty decree of Natural Law had come; the Planet had inclined and in the ever advancing tide of Evolution of Earth, its Race must change to make room for a better one. The edict was recognized that this wicked Race should be destroyed, for they knew every secret of the angels, every oppressive and secret power of Satan, and every power of those who commit sorcery, as well as of those who make molten images, in the whole Earth.

It is from the Fourth Race that the early Aryans got their Knowledge of the most wonderful things, such as flying air vehicles, and instructions in the great arts and sciences so valuable to humanity. We find in the allegory of Moses piloting the Children of Israel out of Egypt, and the destruction of the Egyptians and their Pharoah into the Red Sea, a version of the Legends told of the Atlanteans; an ancient commentary reads as follows. "And the great King of the Dazzling Race, the chief of all the Yellow-faced was sad, seeing the sins of the Black faced. He sent his Vimanas zeppelins (i.e., air ships) to all his brother Chiefs of other Nations and Tribes, with pious men within, saying pre- pare, arise ye men of the Good Law, and cross the Land while it is yet dry. The Lords of the storm are approaching. One night and two days only shall the Lords of the Dark Face, the sorcerers, Black magicians live on the patient Earth. She is doomed and the evil must descend with her. The Lords of the evil Eye are strong, they are versed in Astra, the highest magical knowledge. Come and use your magical powers to counteract those of the sorcerers. Let every Lord of the dazzling face, cause the Air Vehicles of every Lord of the Dark Face to come into his hands, lest the sorcerers should by its means escape from the waters and save his wicked followers. May every Yellow Face send sleep from himself to hypnotize every Black Face. Let even the sorcerers avoid pain and suffering. But let none escape their destiny. And may every Yellow Face offer of his Blood to the speaking animal of a Black Face lest he awaken his Master. The hour has struck, the Black Night is ready." The Great fell upon his dazzling face and wept. The Nations had now crossed the dry lands. They were beyond the Water Mark. The Kings reached them in their Air Ships and led them East and North. Meteors showed on the lands of the Black Face but they slept. The Waters rose and covered the valleys from one end of the Earth to the other. High lands remained and there dwelt those who escaped. The sincere ones called the straight eyed. Some of the more powerful of the sorcerers awoke and pursued the Sons of Wisdom; their heads and chests soared high above the waters, and the commentary says they continued their chase for three Lunar terms, until the waves finally reached them and they perished to the last man, the soil sinking under their feet and the Earth engulfing those who had so terribly desecrated her.

The earliest pioneers of the Fourth Race were not the Atlanteans. Lemuria was a gigantic Land, it covered the whole area from the foot of the Himalayas which separated it from the inland Sea, rolling its waves over what is now Tibet, Mongolia and the Great Gobi, then stretching South 'cross what is known to us as Southern India, Ceylon and Sumatra, embracing on its way Madagascar on the right and Australia and Tasmania on the left. And from Australia it ex- tends far into the Pacific Ocean beyond Easter Island; and what are now the Polar Regions were formerly the earliest of the Seven Cradles of Humanity, and the tomb of the bulk of the mankind of that region during the Third Race, when the gigantic Continent of Lemuria began separating into smaller continents.

-25-

The Easter Island relics are the most astonishing and eloquent memorials of the Primitive Giants. They are grand and mysterious, and one can recognize the features of the type and character attributed to the Fourth Race Giants. There were Giants in the days of old, of which we have proof in fossil remains, and the historical works of China are full of such reminiscences about the Fourth Race Giants. The mental visual perception, or the Third Eye, lasted until nearly the end of the Fourth Race, when its function died out, owing to the materiality and depraved condition of mankind. Strictly speaking it is only from the time of the Atlantean Brown and Yellow Giant Races, that one should speak of Man, since it was the Fourth Race only, which was the first completely human species, much larger in size than we are now. Thus with the Fourth Race we reached the purely human period.

Those who were hitherto Semi-Divine Beings, self-imprisoned in bodies which were human only in appearance, became physiologically changed, and took unto themselves wives who were entirely human and fair to look upon, but in whom lower, more material, though Sidereal Beings had incarnated. These beings in female forms, were the Liliths of Jewish tradition. They were credited with the art of walking in the air, and of the greatest kindness to mortals, but with no mind, only animal instinct.

Previous to the Fourth Race, language was monosyllabilic, but in this Race became agglutinative, to be followed in the Fifth, by the more highly developed and agreeable inflectional speech. Language is coeval with reason, and could never have been developed before man became one with the informing principle. In them Thought and Language are identical but words are sometimes inadequate for our deepest Spiritual Thoughts, generated by the Inner Vision.

When the Fourth Race arrived at its middle age, the inner vision had to be awakened and acquired by artificial stimuli, the process of which (now the lost word), was known to the old Sages. This vision could henceforth be acquired only through training and initiation in the case of natural born magicians, sensitives and mediums as they are now called. The Third Eye soon disappeared. During the activity of the inner man, that is in spiritual trances or visions, this eye swells and expands. The Initiate sees and feels it and regulates his action accordingly. The undefiled Lanoo need feel no danger; but he who keeps himself not in purity, will receive no help from the Deva Eye.

There were human creatures in those early days of the hermaphrodites with four Auras, and three Eyes. These were symbolized in India, by some of the Idols of their exoteric Gods; and in Greece by the Giant Cyclops; the Deva Eye exists no more.

For the majority of mankind this third eye is dead and acts no longer; but it has a witness in the Pineal Gland. There is much to be said in regard to how its power was lost, and how it is to be restored.

We find a suggestion in the Secret Doctrine where the Fourth Race is symbolized by a Priapean Monster. A division arose between the Sons of the Fourth Race as soon as the first Temple and Halls of Initiation had been erected, under the guidance of the Sons of God, allegorized by the Sons of Jacob. That there were two schools of magic, and that the Orthodox Levites did not belong to the Holy One, is shown in the words pronounced by the dying Jacob. He said Dan should be a Serpent that biteth the horses Heels, so that the Rider shall fall backwards - this meaning that he will teach candidates Black Magic.

The great Science of Wisdom, in early days was called Magic; and could be used for good or evil, according to the trend of the individual character possessing it, - quite the same at the present time, but what have become secrets in our Race was public property in the Third Race.

Before the real advent of the Fourth Race, the majority of mankind had fallen into iniquity and sin - save the Sons of the Fire-Mist - and gradually humanity decreased in stature. Then came the Atlanteans, whose giant physical beauty and strength, reached their climax in accordance with Evolutionary Law, toward the middle period of the Fourth Sub Race. But the last survivors of the Fair Child of the White Island had perished, ages before Lemuria's elect had taken shelter on the sacred Island; now the fabled "Shamballah" in the Gobi Desert, while some of their accursed races, separating from the main stock, now lived in the jungles and under ground (cave men), and then the Yellow Fourth Race became in its turn black with sin.

The near future of our Race will find definite proof of the Sunken Continent; presumably the Desert of Gobi will yield the first Treasures of that proof, as the Ocean bottoms are covered by thousands of feet of chalky deposit. (Proof of this deposit having existed during the submersions found in the chalky straits of Palestine, the coast of Asia, etc.).

About the middle period of the Fourth Race, the Earth from Pole to Pole, had changed her face for the third time, the Demi-Gods of the Third had made room for the Semi-Demons of the Fourth Race; the White Island had veiled her face, her children now lived on the Black Land.

It is said the Fourth was born under Soma, the Moon. Every active power of the Earth comes to her from one of the Seven Lords; and it is through Venus that the Hermaphrodites of the Third Race descended.

From the first Sweat-Born in the middle Third Race, when androgynous beings began to evolve into separate males and females, and when the sam Law led them to reproduce their kind as at present, then only was speech developed; but only an experimental form, and the whole Human Race was at that time of one language.

In the Greek Mythology, the quarrel of Latona with Niobe, the mother of seven sons and seven daughters, symbolizes much of the early history of mankind. Niobe represents the Fourth Race with her Seven Sub Races and Seven Branches. Ancient writers distinguished between Lemuria and Atlantis, by calling one the North Hypoborean, and the other the South Hypoborean Continents. And the Golden Apples carried away by Hercules, were in Hypoborean Atlantis, at the distribution of the Children of Niobe by Latonia; the fable relates that Niobe shed never ceasing tears. This refers to the Atlantean Continent being submerged and the doom of its last Generations. One of the aspects of Latona is so Mystic that we find it represented in Revelations as the Woman Clothed With The Sun.

We are told that the wrath of the Sons of God, or Will and Yoga, at seeing

the steady degredation of the Atlanteans was great, which compels us to specu-
late what might be the state of mind they would assume at the present time in
viewing the degredation, destruction, cruelty, crime, black magic and all the
evil selfishness of our present Fifth Race. Why the wrath of the united Gods
is so patient and slow, tolerating so long this continued and increased wicked-
ness is a query for no ordinary mind. All the fables of Greece would be found
to be built on historical facts, if that history had only passed to posterity
unadulterated by Myths. The "One-eyed" Cyclopes, the Giants fabled as the sons
of Coelus and Terra - three in number, according to Hesoid - were the last
three sub-races of the Lemurians, the "One-eyed" referring to the Wisdom-eye;
for the two front eyes were fully developed as physical organs only in the beginning of the Fourth Race. The allegory of Ulysses, whose companions were
devoured, while the King Ithica is based upon the psycho-physiological atrophy
of the Third Eye. And the adventure of Ulysses with Cyclops, a savage gigantic
Race, is an allegorical record of the gradual passage from the Cyclopean Civilization of stone and collossal buildings, to the more sensual and physical
culture of the Atlanteans, which finally caused the last of the Third Race to
loose their all-penetrating Spiritual Eye. And Apollo, whose duty it was to
punish desecration, killed them - his shafts representing human passion, fiery
and lethal.

The three Giants of Mythology also represent the three Polar Lands which
have changed form several times at each cataclysm, or disappearance of one Continent to make room for another.

The whole Globe is convulsed periodically, and has been thus changed since
the appearance of the First Race four times. But these convulsions do not alter
the Polar Lands. From the first appearance of the vast Continent of Lemuria,
the three Polar Giants have been imprisoned in their Circle by Cronus. They
are surrounded by a Wall of Bronze, and their exit is by the Gate of the Seas.
All these historical facts become in later days theological Dogmas. Selfish,
ambitious men of a small sub-race, born but yesterday, and one of the latest
issues of the Aryan stock, took upon themselves to overturn the religious
thought and truth of the world, and succeeded. For nearly two thousand years,
we have been the blind and ignorant, allowing ourselves to be dominated and led
by those more ignorant, selfish and unscrupulous than the multitudes, with the
result that we today are landed in the ditch of Chaos, few knowing how to ex-
tricate themselves, having been so long impressed with the belief of a Personal
Satan, and a Personal God. In the language of a great author: "The multitudes
have only been told what the Deity is not."

All forms which now people the Earth are so many variations on basic types
originally thrown off by the man of the Third and Fourth Round; the basic types
were very few in number compared with the multitude of organisms to which they
ultimately gave rise, but the general unity of type, has never-the-less been
preserved throughout the Ages. The great economy of Nature does not sanction
the coexistence of several utterly opposed, ground plans of evolution on one
Planet, but once the general drift of Occult explanation is formulated and all
the vast wave of Life upon the Globe is under the mighty Law of Evolution,
pushed onward toward the higher Life upon the Globe.

Each Entity must have won for itself the right of becoming Divine through self-experience. It is time we expand in Soul and in Mind; our Consciousness seeking that which is Eternal Life beyond the bounds of Matter.

In the study of the Races of Mankind, we must bear in mind that Races, like individuals, differ in spiritual gifts, as in color, in stature, etc. Among some, Seership naturally prevails; among others mediumship. Some are addicted to sorcery, and transmit its secret rules of practice from generation to generation with a wide range of psychic phenomena, from their intimate practical knowledge of magnetism and electricity and familiarity with its effects in and upon the animal kingdom and mankind. Summing it all up in a few words this knowledge is magic or spiritual wisdom - Nature - the material Ally, pupil and servant of the Magician.

One common vital principle pervades all things, and this is controllable by the perfected Human Will. And it is this principle that was dominated by the Evil Fourth Race people, for selfish purposes, and which eventually wrought their complete destruction. The periods of the Great Root Races are divided from each other, by great convulsions of Nature, and by great Geological changes.

At the time of the Fourth Race flourished, Europe was not in existence, and the Fourth Race Continent had not appeared at the time the Third Race flourished; and both of these continents have no existence at the present time. Each Race is cut off in this way, at its appointed time, some survivors remaining in parts of the world, but not the proper home of their Race, and they exhibit a tendency to decay and barbarism with more or less rapidity.

Early in the Fourth Race Cycle, we are told that the Great Continent of Atlantis showed symptoms of sinking, a process that continued down to nearly 12,000 years ago, when its last Island Possidonis went down with a crash.

During the destruction of Atlantis, the majestic peaks of the mighty Alps were elevated by the crushing of the Earth crust at that point.

The great evil of our egoistic selfish Fifth Race will be arrested, the same as that of its predecessors, when physical intellect, which is unguarded by elevated morality, shall retard Spiritual Advancement.

The great Natural Law provides for the violent repression of Evil, and there are analogies between the Life of a Nation and that of an individual; but both are governed by inexorable Law. Over the events of Life we may have control, but none whatever over the Law of its progress.

There is a Geometry that applies to Nations, an equation of their Curves, of advances that no mortal man can touch; and there is a Destiny that shapes our lives, far beyond our own mortal efforts.

KRIYASHAKTI

The Third Root Race began by creating through Kriyashakti and ended by generating its species in the present way.

Magic, the science of hidden mysteries is coeval (same age) with this Race. The power of Kriyashakti should be exercised in the projection of the Mayave Rupa (the double) - the power of producing forms on the objective plane through the potency of and through Ideation and Will, from invisible indestructible matter, to produce emanations; acquiring the gift of Kriyashakti is the direct result of that power, an effect that depends upon our own actions. This power is inherent in us owing to our descent from the one Primordial principle, the Infinite Power or Potency.

The first step then in Kriyashakti is the use of the imagination to Create a perfect model in detail, of what you desire, then bring the Will into action, transferring the form to the objective world. This is creating by Kriyashakti. Christian Science methods etc.

The Mind Born Sons of the early Third Race were the fruits of Kriyashakti. This Third Race is sometimes called collectively the Sons of Passive Yoga. In its early existence Sons of Wisdom incarnated in this Root Race and produced by Kriyashakti a progeny called the Sons of the Fire Mist. They were a conscious production as a portion of the Race was already animated with the Divine Spark of superior spiritual Intelligence.

This progeny was not a Race but a wondrous Being (presumably a Planetary Group Soul), a nursery for future Human Adepts born in an immaculate way. Kriyashakti is a Mysterious Power of Thought which enables it to produce external perceptible, phenomenal results.

By its own inherent Energy, any idea will manifest itself externally if one's attention is Deeply concentrated upon it.

This mysterious and Divine power, latent in the will of every man, which, if not called to life, quickened and developed by Yoga training, remains dormant and atrophies with, perhaps, the exception of one in a million.

The Third Race was created, not begotten, and Creation is the result of Will acting on phenomenal Matter. The first were Shadows, the second the Sweat Born, the Third the Egg Born and the Holy Ones. The Fourth were the children of the Padmapani or Chenristi - (Women were created by Will before they were naturally born from the Hermaphrodites).

Kriyashakti is Will and Yoga. Semen is the projection into matter of the individual sexual Will. Kriyashakti is the Germ of active energy; Man projects the essence of the Creative energy over the Woman; she experiences the thrill of Physical Union by Thought. Shakti, Supreme Creative Power, product of mental and sexual centers - an Aspect of Spirit.

USE OF IN ATLANTIS

Also by present day Black Magicians.
Universal active Female energy. Kriya - Power of Thought.
Shakti, synthesized force, the Crown of the Astral Light.
Woman said to be fated gift to man - her apparition on Earth a signal for every kind of Evil. Races lived happily before her appearance, free from dis-

ease and suffering. She caused the theft of the Divine Fire. The Light that Shineth in Darkness is Woman.

Hessoid says the Immortals made the Race of the Golden Age and the Silver Age, i.e., First and Second Races. Jupiter made the Generation of Bronze, an admixture of two elements. The curse on man came with the formation of Woman according to the Kabalah. The Allegory of Adam being driven away from the Tree of Life means Esoterically, that the newly separated Race abused and dragged down the mystery of Life into the region of animalism and bestiality.

That man was cursed by the formation of woman was the view of the Church Fathers, but it is not Esoteric teaching. The curse did not begin with the formation of either man or woman, but their separation was a natural consequence of Evolution, but the breaking of the Law was the curse. And Exoteric Christianity everywhere is only ceremonial Magic with its terrible effects. Read Chapter XVII of Revelation and learn the mystery of the Woman and the Beast.

Exoteric barbarous idolatrous faiths have ever stained and obliterated Truth with human Blood.

To accept the Drama of humanity as written in Genesis, it was the Lord God who caused all the mischief. He said it was not good for man to be alone. He made Woman and brought her unto Man. All Evil necessary that self-conscious Life may be Immortal.

> Egyptian Symbol 25,000 years -
> Cambyses saw same -
> Lanka -

The Giants of Genesis are the Historical Atlanteans of Lanka and the Greek Titans.

BRONZE AGE

Each Race is divided into Four Ages - Gold, Silver, Brass and Iron.

Esoterically there are three divisions of the Race in Color; the Red-Yellow, the Black and the Brown-White. There are three fundamental elements of Color in the Human Organism - Red, Yellow and Black, which, mixed in variable quantities with the white of the tissues, give rise to the numerous shades of coloring or complexion seen in the human family. The Aryan Race now varying from dark brown, almost black, red brown, yellow down to the whitest creamy color, are never-the-less all of one and the same stock. The Fifth Root Race, the first solid human race appearing about the middle of the Third Root Race was light yellow in color after its fall into generation. A portion of the Fourth Race became Black with Sin Shiva, changing them into red-yellow, of which the red Indian and Mongolians are the descendants, and finally into born white races, which now, together with the Yellow Races, form the grand bulk of Humanity.

-31-

THE RACES OF MANKIND

FIFTH RACE

By

Dr. H. L. Henderson

How long has it taken the world to become what it is now. Students of Occult Law believe that through the countless millions of years of intelligent primeval substance, many humanities differing from our present mankind as greatly as the humanity which will evolve millions of years hence, will differ from our present Races.

These primitive and far distant humanities are denied, because the Geologists think they have left no tangible relics of themselves, as all trace of them is swept away and therefore they never existed; yet their relics are to be found. But even if they were never to be met with, there would be no reason to say that such humanities did not exist. They were Psychic natures enshrined in forms of indestructible Primeval Matter, and were the real forefathers of our Fifth Race.

The Earth and Sun, Moon and Planets all have their growth, changes, development and gradual evolution. Why should not mankind be also under this Universal Law? We are at present near the mid-point of our Sub-Race of the Fifth Root Race, at our acme of materiality, egoism and selfishness; and while the animal propensities, though more refined, are none the less developed than in the density of the Fourth Race; and these animal propensities are most marked in so-called civilized countries. And such conditions will continue until the Spiritual Intuitions of Mankind are fully developed.

We must cast off our thick coats of matter, and begin acting from within, instead of ever following impulses from without produced by our physical senses and gross selfish body. Until then the only palliatives for the Evils of Life are Union and Harmony, Altruism in acts, and not in Name. The suppression of one single bad cause will suppress many bad effects and additional causes of mischief in a world so full of Evil and Woe.

Mankind is its own Saviour or destroyer. There is nothing gained by accusing the Gods, Fates or providence for the apparent injustice that regins in the midst of Humanity. But there is that mysterious something that leads on unerring through ways unmarked, from guilt to <u>punishment</u> and just such now are the ways in which great European nations are moving onward, and something must be born of the struggle.

Every Nation has its Exoteric Cycles depending upon Sidereal Motions, and

-32-

it is neither Prevision nor Prophecy, it is simply Knowledge and mathematically correct computations, which enabled the Wise Ones to foretell in the last Century, that England was on the eve of a catastrophe, and France also was nearing such a point of her cycle and that Europe in general was on the eve of a cataclysm, to which her own Racial Karma has led her.

Eastern Initiates maintain that they have preserved Records of Racial developemnts, and of events of Universal import ever since the beginning of the Fourth Race. Their knowledge of events preceding that Epoch being Traditional.

The Secret Doctrine is the accumulated Wisdom of the Ages, and its Cosmogony alone, is the most stupenduous and elaborate of all systems. But such is the power of the Mysterious Occult Symbolism, that the Facts which have actually occupied countless generations of Initiated Seers and Prophets, to set down and explain in a most bewildering series of evolutionary progress, - which really does not explain but confuses the minds of the masses, - could all be recorded upon a very few pages of Geometrical Signs and Glyphs, i.e., Symbology.

This is the Soul of Things, but Modern Science believes not in the Soul of Things, and has ever rejected the whole system of ancient cosmogony. This system is an uninterrupted Record, covering thousands of Generations of Seers, whose respective experiences were made to test and verify the Traditions passed on Orally, by one early Race to another, the Teachings of the Higher and Exalted Beings who watched over the childhood of Humanity.

For long ages the Wise Men of the Fifth Race of the stock saved from the last cataclysm passed their lives in learning, checking, testing and verifying in every department of Nature, the traditions of old, by the independent visions of Adepts. No vision of one was accepted until confirmed by others of Centuries of experience. The Universe with everything in it is called Maya, because all therein is temporary from the firefly to the Sun; and its conscious beings are as unreal as itself. And everything throughout the Kingdom is Conscious. Where we have no right to say it does not exist. Do not perceive consciousness.

And the Universe is guided from within Outward. Cruel Law is eternal, working from Cycle to Cycle midst all the Nations of the World.

And thus the tenets of Reincarnation came to our Fifth Race Aryans. From their predecessors of the Fourth Race Atlanteans, they had piously preserved the teachings which told them how their parents' Root Race, becoming, with every generation more arrogant, owing to the acquisition of superhuman powers, had been gradually gliding toward its end. These records reminded them of the giant intellect of the preceeding races, as well as of their giant size; and we find the repetition of these records in every Age of History.

During the days of Alexander the Great, we read of Midas being told of a Continent that once existed in times of old, so immense that Asia, Europe and Africa seemed like poor islands compared with it; and it produced animals and plants of gigantic magnitude - our mammoth trees relics. Men grew to double the size at that time and lived to be twice as old. They could perform a

-33-

journey from what we know as the Sahara Desert, to the lands which now rest in dreamless sleep at the bottom of the Waters of the Gulf of Mexico, and the Caribbean Sea.

Events which were only written in Human Memory, but which were religiously transmitted from one generation to another, and from Race to Race, have been preserved by constant tradition in the Book Volume of the Human Brain through countless Aeons, with more truth and accuracy than by any written document or record. The physical brain may forget events within the scope of one terrestrial life, but the bulk of collective recollections can never desert the Divine Soul within us; it forms our thought body. Its whispers may be too soft, the sound of its words too far away to be perceived by our physical senses, yet the shadows of Events that Were, and the shadows of Events that are to Come, is within the perceptive power; and it is this Soul Voice which tells more by tradition, than is written in History. It says the Kings of Light have departed in wrath, for the sins of men have become so black that the Earth quivers in Great Agony.

One of the oldest Nations of our Fifth Race is the Chinese, and they reverence as symbols the Serpent and the Dragon. All the learned people of antiquity reverence as symbols the Serpent and the Dragon; all but the Christians. They choose to forget the Brazen Serpent of Moses; and the supposed sayings of Christ "Be ye wise as Serpents and harmless as Doves" - here serpents symbolize the learned and wise Adepts and the Dove the Divine Feminine principle. The Yellow Dragon is revered by the Chinese as a Symbol. The great philosopher Ivan Ying Tu, says His wisdom and virtue are unfathomable. He does not seek company, he is an escetic. He feeds in the pure water of wisdom, and disports in the clear water of Life- the Dragon Regenerative. Reading from Commentary 20 of the Ancient Book of Dzyan, we find that our present Fifth Race, in our first half of duration onward, on the new ascending Arc of the Cycle are between the 1st and 2nd.

As the Races came down, nascent mankind was there devoid of the intellectual brain element as it was on its descending line, coming out from spirituality in quest of the Tree of Knowledge on this terrible man-bearing planet. And as we are therefore devoid of the Spiritual Element as a Race, replacing it by the Intellectual and an unfortunate and dangerous principle of egoism.

But we are cycling onward on the Spiritual side and the full development of Manas as a direct Ray from the Universal. A Ray unimpeded by matter will finally be reached, restoring our Spirituality plus a lofty intelligence.

Human Races are born one from the other; grow, develop, become old, and die. Since the beginning of the Atlantean Race many million years have passed away, yet we find the last of the Atlanteans still mixed up with the Aryan element - more markedly so about 11,000 years ago. This shows the enormous overlapping of one Race over the Race which succeeds it, though in character and external type and the elder loses and assumes the new features of the younger Race. And even now, under our very eyes, a new Race is in preparation in America. This transformation will take place and has already commenced.

Plato tells us that the Priests of Sais said to Solon: "You one time inhabited your country and from whom you are descended, though only a remnant now remains. This Race was the Seventh Sub-Race of the Atlanteans, from which prodeded Egypt, Greece and the Phoenicians.

Plato, when a child, was told the story of Atlantis by his Grand Sire Critias, aged ninety, who in his youth had been told of it by Solon, who was one of the Seven Sages of Greece.

The Fifth Race was in its infancy when Atlantis went down. And alone the handful of those Elect whose Divine Instructors had gone to inhabit the Sacred Island, remained faithful, and joined with the nascent Fifth Race; and when the poles moved for the Fourth Time, those who had separated from the Fourth Race were protected. Alone the ungodly Atlanteans perished and were seen no more. Few men remained, some Yellow, some Black - Brown and Red. The Moon Colored or Primitive Divine Stock were gone. The Fifth produced from the Holy Stock remained, and we were ruled over by the First Divine Kings.

The Serpents who re-descended, who made peace with the Fifth Race, teaching and instructing it. The Great Dragon symbolizes the Deluge of the Third or Lemurian Race. The Commentary says, the Great Dragon has respect but for the Serpents of Wisdom, namely, the Adepts or Wise Men of the Race. Knowledge and Wisdom alone are ALL in times of crisis and the great summing up of the harvest of Nations and of Individuals.

It was the belief of all antiquity, by Pagan and Christian, that the earliest mankind was a race of Giants. Certain excavations in America, in mounds and caves have already, in isolated cases, yielded groups of skeletons of nine and twelve feet high. These belong to tribes of the early Fifth Race now regenerated to an average size of between five and six feet.

In Sinnett's Occult World, the description of a cavern in the Himalayas filled with relics of giant human and animal bones is a further proof of the Giants of the early part of our great Aryan Fifth Race. Also we learn by comparison and study that the final adjustment of the human organism became perfected and symmetrical only in the Fifth Race.

The duration of the periods that separate in space and time the Fourth and Fifth Races in the historical, or even legendary, calculations is too tremenduous to even enter into any detailed account of same. For during the course of the Post-deluvian Ages, which were marked at certain periodical epochs by the most terrible cataclysms, too many Races and Nations were born and disappeared almost without leaving a trace for any one to offer any description of value concerning the same. Only in symbolism can the history of the planet be traced.

When we consider the collosal effort of all Nature's combined force in building and sustaining the Planet, under the struggling Life-wave, we can fully realize more and more the fact that Humanity must either be the Miller, or that shifting grain ground exceedingly fine by the Stupenduous Machiners of the Law, and the escape from between the Mighty Wheels, and from being the Grain to being the Miller, can only be accomplished by Humanity itself, by mind and Soul expansion into the Consciousness of the Universal.

-35-

Knowledge and Wisdom are the only gold of existence worth possessing, and belong the same to Woman as to Man. "Seek and ye shall find."

The Rig Veda, the oldest known record of the Primordial Teachings of our Fifth Race, speaks of Two more Races to come, allegorizing them by the Seven Strams; but only profound study can master the secret meaning of the relations between the Heavenly Man - the Spiritual Man sacrificed for the production of the Universe and all in it - and the terrestrial Mortal Man hidden in the philosophy of this statement. "The Spiritual or Heavenly Man has Seven enclosing logs of fuel, and Thrice Seven layers of fuel. When the Gods performed the Sacrifice they bound the Man as the Victim." There is nothing said about the unbinding or release of the victim. Mankind must develop the God-power and effect their own release.

Observe that those who wrote, or recorded the Vedas were the Initiates or Rishes of our Fifth Race and they wrote at the time Atlantis had already gone down. Atlantis being the fourth continent that appeared, but the Third that disappeared. (The First remains intact). And we are told that the Fifth Race was guided and instructed after the last deluge. Presumably it departed from the Wisdom of those Instructors - if present conditions are any guide or example for speculation.

But it is said that we of this egoistic Fifth Race generated our heaviest Karma as Monads of the Fourth Race (Racial Karma is heaviest now); in other words we are a reincarnation of the Atlanteans, and must reap our past and present Karma, a word of many meanings, one of which is the Law of Ethical Causation, the effect of an act produced egotistically in the face of the Great Law of Harmony, which is based upon and dependent upon the noble principle of Altruism. There can be no Harmony without Altruism, and the Law of Karma is inextricably interwoven with that of Reincarnation, and it is only this doctrine that can reconcile us to the terrible apparent injustice of Life. For as one observes the inequalities of birth and fortune, intellect and capacities, when one sees honor paid to fools and profligates, on whom fortune has heaped her favors, by mere privilege of birth, and their nearest neighbor possessed of intellect and noble virtues far more deserving, but perishing for want of sympathy and understanding. To know all this and be forced to turn away helpless to relieve the seeming undeserved suffering of aching hearts and cries of pain.

But for the Blessed Knowledge of Karmic Law, Soul alone could not prevent us from cursing Life, Mankind and all the Creators; and the individual today, who can indifferently and selfishly smile, remaining cold and calm over the present environment of this Man-ruled world of war and crime, in which we are forced to live, is utterly devoid of Soul, filled with selfishness, vanity and self-satisfied egoism; and they should dwell in the shell of a Clam at Low Tide, during their next incarnation. Better make a log-chain creep with Soul indignation rather than exist in cold-blooded indifference, and luke-warmness depending upon the pulpit and personal adornment to satisfy.

Our Fifth Race has been much deceived and misled, the non-initiated knowing of but one deluge, looked after by an old myth called Noah; and knowledge of Law by the enlightenment of Woman alone, can ever restore the Real in Truth.

From reliable authority, we are told that Religion is a wide prudential feeling grounded on more calculation. So-called Christian Nations having burdened themselves with it, feel bound to poetize and defend it, at the expense of all other beliefs and good common sense. But it was not so with the Ancient Nations. For them the passage entrance, and the sarcophagus in the King's chamber meant Regeneration, NOT generation. It was the most solemn Symbol, a Holy of Holies, wherein were created Immortal Hierophants and Sons of God, NEVER mortal men and sons of lust and flesh, as now in the hidden sense of the Semitic Kabalist.

The reason for the difference in the views of the Two Races is easy to account for; The Aryan Hindu belongs to the oldest race now on earth. The Semites, Hebrew to the latest, the former nearly One Million years old; the latter a tribe descended from the Chaldeans of India, born about 8,000 B.C., an artificial Aryan Race, Jew, Parsia, Armenian; three Races of the Same Aryan Caucasian types. From the Seven primitive types of the Fifth Race, there now remain on Earth but Three; Caucasian, Mongolian, and Ethiopian. All existing individuals of the species can be ranged around these types.

After the submersion of the last remnant of the Atlantean Race some 12,000 years ago, an IMPENETRABLE VEIL OF SECRECY was thrown over the Occult and Religious Mysteries, lest they should be shared and desecrated by the unworthy - which they have been, - (Who the judge?). But their Dogmas and Tenets, being ALL SYMBOLIZED and left to the sole guardianship of Parable and Allegory, have been forgotten, and hence the meaning has become perverted; however, one finds the Hermaphrodites in the Scriptures and Traditions of nearly all nations.

Under the cover of this secrecy, the Fifth Race was led to the re-establishment of the Religious Mysteries in which ancient Truths might be taught to the coming generations, under the veil of Allegory and Symbolism.

Behold the Egyptian Sphinx, the riddle of the Ages, an imperishable witness to the Evolution of the Human Races from the androgynous state. Divine Wisdom incarnating on Earth, forced to taste the bitter fruit of Personal Experience of pain and suffering, generated on Earth only under the shadow of the Tree of Knowledge of good and evil, a secret first known only to the Elohim.

The Great Sages who Taught the Fifth, after having instructed the two preceeding Races, had Ruled during the Divine Dynasties, had sacrificed themselves to be reborn, under various circumstances, for the good of mankind and for its salvation at critical periods. Until, in their last incarnations, they became only the part of a part on Earth, though, de facto, the One Supreme in Nature.

In rapid progress of Anthropomorphism and Idolatry led the early Fifth, as it had already led the Fourth Race, into sorcery again, and the Black Magicians inaugurated the birth and evolution of the Sacerdotal Castes, finally leading the World into all these Exoteric Religions which have been invented to satisfy the depraved taste of the "Hoi Pelloi" and the ignorant, for ritualistic pomp and materialization of the ever Immaterial and Unknowable Principle.

But we are told that this was a certain improvement on the Atlantean sorcery. If the present condition of our Fifth Race under the exoteric False

Religions are an improvement on the dire Atlantean evil sorcery, then let us rejoice that the Atlanteans went down; and may the old Earth again heave, and rock, and tremble, to swallow up its atrocious progeny, burying them so deep beneath the briny waves that they can never be again born to curse the patient Land.

The Religion of the Early Fifth Race was Fire Worship, and when the Race again overcomes Black Magic and falsity, to it we will return. For it is the only Religious Philosophy not at variance with Science, and it is the basic foundation of Freemasonry and of Roman Catholic knowledge. The tenets of Reincarnation and the Fire Philosophy, came to the Fifth Race Aryans from the Fourth Race Atlanteans. They had faithfully preserved the Teachings which told them how their Parent Root Race, becoming with every generation more arrogant, owing to the acquisition of Superhuman Powers, had been gradually gliding toward its end. And our own arrogant Fifth Race, with its Giant Intellectual Capacities, and selfish cunning, is just as surely sliding and gliding on to its own destruction; the subtle gliding can even now be easily discerned, and the toboggan crash is not in the far away future.

The civilization of the Atlanteans was greater than that of the Egyptians, and it was their degenerate descendants who built the first Pyramids. According to the best modern calculations there are no less than 500,000,000 stars of various magnitude within the range of the best telescopes, and the distances between them are incalculable. Is then our little Earth a grain of sand in an Infinite Sea-Shore, the only center of Intelligent Life? Our own Sun itself 1,300,000 times larger than our Planet, sinks into insignificance beside the giant Sun Sirius, and the latter is again dwarfed by other Luminaries in Infinite Space.

Reflecting upon these vast conceptions, the self-centered idea of Jehovah being the special guardian of a small and obscure semi-nomadic tribe is tolerable beside that idea which confines sentient existence to our small Globe, that has not yet passed the stage of periodically changing its skin. The primary reason for this lack of understanding was first, astronomical ignorance on the part of the early Christians, combined with exaggerated egoism (a crude of selfishness); and second, the dread that if the hypothesis of millions of other inhabited globes were accepted the crushing rejoinder would ensue.

Was there then a revelation to each World? Involving the idea of the Son of God eternally going the rounds, as it were? Happily, it is now unnecessary to waste time and energy in proving the existence of other worlds. All intelligent people admit it, and this proves the evolution of preceeding Races.

Under Mercury was the Fifth Race evolved; for the development of Mind was its chief work. Thus the Planet of Knowledge shed its rays over its Birth Hour. The home of this Race was established in Central Asia, and thereafter a long halt came, then came the first emigration, perhaps some 850,000 years ago, of the First Sub Race called the Aryan, although this name applied to the whole Fifth Race.

They were forced Southward across the mighty Belt of the Himalayas and settled in North India. These Aryans received the Zodiac directly from the

-38-

Sons of Will and Yoga, and they brought from Central Asia the Senzar language, said to be the secret sacerdotal tongue.

If we had the time, it would be interesting to trace the Fifth Race off-shoots and their travels.

The Aryo-Semitic crossed the Euphrates into Syria and Arabia, and the Assyrian and Babylonian Empires arose from coalescence with the Turanian and Akadian tribes, and the Phoenicians, Egyptians and ancient Greeks arose from their intermixture with the Seventh Sub Race of Atlanteans. Also some of these off-shoots traveled Eastward mingling with the Mongolians, giving rise to the Manchu Dragon Throne of China. The Irania went North and East - led by Zara-thustra, the Keltic passed Westward, the Teutonic also migrated Westward, oc-cupying all Central Europe, and now spreading over the World, driving before it in North America, the Old Atlantean Stock - the Red Indians - seizing Aus-tralia and New Zealand, remnants of ancient Lemuria, the poor relics of the dying Race vanishing before it.

But high as it has reared its proud head, it too must pass away as Ages roll on their course. Then shall Shaka rise to be the Continent of the new Sixth Root Race, emerging and changing North America. And in America that Race is now forming. It will be the subject of our next Lesson.

****

SIXTH AND SEVENTH

Owing to unknown circumstances there appear from time to time great think-ers, who, devoting their time to single purpose, are able to anticipate the progress of Mankind and produce a philosophy by which important effects are eventually brought about.

But if we look into history we shall clearly see that although the origin of a new opinion may be thus due to a single man, the result which the new opinion produces will depend on the condition of the people among whom it is propagated. If either a religion or a philosophy is too much in advance of a Nation it can do no present service, but must bide its time. This is Cyclic Law. But this Law itself is often defied by human stubbornness. Every science, every creed had its Martyrs, and according to the ordinary course of affairs, a few generations pass away and then there comes a period when these very truths are looked upon as commonplace facts, and a little later there comes another period in which they are declared to be necessary, and even the dullest intellect wonders how they could ever have been denied.

We have already learned that the minds of the present generation are not ready to receive the Truths of Nature's hidden or Occult Laws. But the advanced

-39-

thinkers of the Sixth Root Race will accept esoteric philosophy fully and unconditionally. Meanwhile the generations of our Fifth Race will continue to be led away by prejudice and preconceptions, and materialism will seek to crush the name of Occult Science.

But the hour has now struck to ascertain whether the Walls of the modern Jericho are so impregnable that no blast of the trumpet of Occult Law and Truth can make them crumble. Old and time honored errors become every day more glaring and self evident and stand arrayed in battle order, marshalled by blind conservatism, conceit and prejudice; they are constantly on the watch, ready to strangle every truth which, awakening from its age long sleep, happens to knock for admission. Such has been the case ever since Man became an animal.

Occult Science recognizes Seven Cosmic Elements, four entirely physical and the Fifth, which is Ether and semi-material will become visible in the Air in the near future and dominate over the other Elements of One Round - or Life Cycle. (Aviation). The remaining two are as yet absolutely beyond the range of human perception, but will appear during the Sixth and Seventh Races.

The Fifth Universal Cosmic Principle, of Father-Mother of antiquity from which proceeds human mind is cosmically a radiant, cool, diathermanous (Transmitting radiant heat) plastic matter, creative in its physical nature and immutable in its higher principles; in conjunction with radiant heat it recalls dead worlds to life. In its higher aspect it is the Soul of the World, in its lower, the Destroyer.

The word Dzyan means the one Real Magical Knowledge or Occult Wisdom which, dealing with eternal truths and primal causes, becomes almost Omnipotence when applied in the right direction. The mighty etheric Currents are the Steed, and Thought is the Rider. It passes like lightning through the Fiery Clouds or Cosmic Mist. Its voice calls the innumerable sparks and joins them together.

Occult Philosophy divulges few of its most important and vital mysteries. It drops them like precious Pearls one by one, far and wide apart - No one book has them - and even this only when forced to do so by the evolutionary tidal wave that carries Humanity on and on slowly, silently but steadily toward the dawn of the great Sixth Race of Mankind. For if they fall into the hands of the selfish Cains of the human Race they are more liable to become a curse than a blessing.to humanity. Our illusion is so great that we have no right to dogmatize about the possible nature of the perceptive faculties of a Sixth Plane Ego. The pure Object apart from Consciousness is unknown to us while living on the plane of the three dimensional World. (Know the dimensional world this century) - With no more than five senses, and no power to divorce our Ego from their thralldom, it is impossible for the personal Ego to break through the carrier which separates it FROM a knowledge of things themselves. The Ego progressing an Arc of ascending subjectivity must exhaust the experience of every plane.

The object of the vast and laborious task of evolving the Universe was the hope of attaining clear self consciousness, a state of which we are unable to form a single concept - being powerless to raise the veil that shrouds the Majesty of the Absolute. Only the liberated spirit is able to faintly realize the nature of the source from whence it sprung, and whither it must eventually return.

Nothing can save those Races that have run their course. Those who have defended themselves most valiantly, Hawaiians or Maories, have been no less decimated than the tribes massacred or tainted by European intrusion. The science of Ethnology will sooner or later be forced to recognize the workings of Karmic Law, and the dying out of the Hawaiians is one of the mysterious problems of the present time; for the time is drawing near when there will remain nothing but three great human types.

Just before the Sixth Root Race dawns there will be only the White Aryan, the Yellow Mongolian and the Ethiopian with their crossings (Atlanto-European, etc.). Redskins, Eskimos, Australians, Polynesians etc., are all dying out. The tide-wave of incarnating Egos has rolled past them to harvest experience in more developed and less senile Stock, and their extinction is a necessity by Law.

Every mixed Race when uniform and settled has been able to play the part of a primary Race in fresh crossings. Mankind in its present state has thus been formed for the greatest part by the successive crossings of a great number of Races. Thus the Americans have become in only three centuries a primary Race temporarily before becoming a Race apart and strongly separated from all other now existing Races; they are in short the Germs of the sixth Sub Race, and in some few hundred years will become most decidedly the pioneers of that Race which must succeed to the present European or Fifth Sub Race in all its new characteristics.

After this, in about 25,000 years, they will launch into preparations for the Seventh Sub-Race.

The first great cataclysms must in time destroy Europe, and still later the whole Aryan Race, affecting both Americas and most of the lands connected with our Continent and Islands. The Sixth Root Race will have appeared on the stage of our Round. It will silently come into existence, so silently that for long Millenniums will its pioneers be regarded as abnormal oddities physically and mentally; peculiar children will grow into peculiar men and women: and as their numbers grow greater with every age, one day they will awake to find themselves in the majority, and present mankind will begin to be regarded as exceptional mongrels until they die out as past Races have done, surviving only in small groups on Islands - the mountain peaks of today - where they will vegetate, degenerate and finally die out, perhaps millions of years hence as the Aztecs, the Nyam, the Korumba, and others have done; these are all remnants of once mighty Races, the recollection of whose existence has entirely died out of the remembrance of modern generations. Just as we shall vanish from the memory of the Sixth Race Humanity. The Fifth will overlap the Sixth Race for many millenniums, changing with it more slowly than its new successor, still changing in stature, general physique and mentality.

Just as the Fourth overlapped our Aryan Race and the Third the Atlanteans, this process of preparation for the great Sixth Race must last throughout the Sixth and Seventh Sub Races. But the last remnants of the Fifth Continent will not disappear until sometime after the birth of the new Race, when another and new dwelling - the Sixth Continent - will have appeared above the new waters on the face of the Globe to receive the great stranger. To this new Continent also will emigrate and settle all those fortunate enough to escape the general disaster.

Nature does not move suddenly, and the final cataclysm will be preceeded by many smaller submersions and destructions, both by wave and volcanic fires. The exultant pulse will beat high in the heart of the Race now in the American zone, but there will be no more Americans when the Sixth Race commences; no more Europeans, for they will have now become a new Race and many new Nations. Yet the Fifth will not die but will survive for a while, over-lapping the new Race for many hundred thousands of years to come, becoming transformed slowly, altered in mentality, general physique and stature.

Mankind will never grow again into giant bodies, as the Lemurians and At- lanteans, because while the evolution of the Fourth Race brought it down to the very bottom of materiality in its physical development, the present Race is on its ascending arc, and the Sixth Race will be rapidly growing out of its bonds of matter and flesh.

Cycles of spirituality will dominate over cycles of matter, and Mind will be fully developed. Humanity is the Child of Cyclic Destiny, and not one of its Units can escape its unconscious mission or get rid of the burden of its co-operative work of Nature. And thus will mankind, Race after Race, perform the appointed Cyclic Pilgrimage.

Climates will, and have already, begun to change; such is the course of Nature under the sway of Law. The Present is the Child of the Past, the Future the begotten of the Present. Thus the Past, Present and Future are the ever- living Trinity in One.

When the Laws of Nature shall be buried in ruins and the last days of the World shall come, the Southern Pole shall crush as it falls, all the regions of Africa, and the North Pole shall overwhelm all the countries beneath its axis. In the 3rd Chapter of the Second Epistle of Peter we read as follows: - "By the Word of God the heavens were of old, and the earth standing out of the water and in the water; whereby the world that then was, being overflowed with water, perished. The heavens being on fire shall be dissolved, and the elements shall melt with fervent heat." Nevertheless we look for new heavens and a new earth. This refers to the destruction of our present Fifth Race by subterranean Fires and inundations, and the appearance of new continents for the new Sixth Root Race; and the minds of those who live at that time shall be awakened and become pellucid as crystal, and those who are thus changed by virtue of that peculiar time shall be as the seeds of other human beings, and shall in time give birth to the Sons of God, born of immaculate parents and known as the Seventh Race. Immaculate conception will then be understood.

The Secret Doctrine teaches us that the Arts, Sciences, Theology and espe- cially the Philosophy of every Nation which preceeded the last universally known but not universal deluge had been recorded ideographically from the primitive oral records of the Fourth Race, and that these were the inheritance of the latter from the early Third Root Race before the allegorical fall. Hence also the Egyptian pillars, the Tablets and even the White oriental porphyry Stone of the Masonic legend, were simply the more or less symbolical and allegorical copies from the primitive records. The Book of Enoch is one of such copies, - very incomplete Chaldean compendium. Enoch is a generic title and his legend is that of several other prophets, Jewish and Heathen, with changes of made-up details.

We read that Enoch and Elijah were taken up to the Heaven World, symboliz- ing a kind of easy death or euthanasia of those who have reached the power and degree, also purification which enables them to die in the physical body and still lead and live a conscious life in the Astral body.

The Pauline expression that "he should not see death" has an esoteric mean- ing; and the mangled biblical hints in regard to the return of Enoch and Elijah at the destruction of evil, signifies esoterically that some of the Great Souls will return in the Seventh Race, when all error will be made away with and the advent of the Truth will be heralded by the Holy Sons of Light.

The chronology and computations of the Brahman Initiates are based upon the Zodiacal records of India and the works of the Great Astronomer and Magic- ian Asuramaya. The Atlantean Zodiacal records cannot err as they were compiled under the guidance of those who first taught Astronomy to mankind, and the a- bove mentioned teacher based all his astronomical works upon very ancient rec- ords, and determined the duration of all past geological and cosmical periods, and the length of all the cycles to come till the end of this life Cycle or the end of the Seventh Race.

Seven means all the mighty hammer of creation called the Swastika, the Alpha and Omega of Universal Creative Force evolving from pure Spirit and end- ing in gross matter. It is also the key to the cycle of Science, Divine and Human, and he who comprehends its full meaning, is forever liberated from the toils of the great Illusion and Deceiver.

The Light that shines from under the Divine Hammer, now degraded into the mallet or gavel of the Grand Masters of Masonic Ladges, is sufficient to dis- sipate the darkness of all human schemes or fiction.

The songs of the three Norse Goddesses to whom the ravens of Odin whispher of the past and future, are all written down on the scrolls of Wisdom, and they repeat in poetic allegory the teachings of the Archaic Ages.

In the summary of Wagner from Asgard and the Gods concerning the renewal of the World, we find a prophecy about the Seventh Race of our Round. It reads as follows - "On the fields of Ida, the field of resurrection, the Sons of the highest Gods assembled and in them their Fathers rose again" - (the Egos of all their past incarnations) - They talked of the Past and the Present, and re- membered the Wisdom and prophecies of their Ancestors which had all been ful- filled. Near them but invisible was the Mighty One who ordains the Eternal Laws that govern the world; they all felt his presence and power. At his com- mand the new Earth rose out of the waters of space. To the South above the field of Ida, were arranged three Heavens, symbolizing the three gradually ascending <u>Globes of our Chain.</u> Then were the Gods enthroned as they used to be and they rejoiced in the restoration of the better time. From Gimels heights the high and pure Seventh Globe, they looked down upon the happy descendants of purified Humanity, and signed to them to climb up higher, to rise to knowledge and wisdom, in piety, and in deeds of Love, step by step, from one heaven to another until they were at last prepared to be united to the Divinities in the great home of All.

It is not in the course of Natural Law that man should become a perfect septenary being before the Seventh Race, and in the Seventh Round. Yet he has all these principles latent in him from his birth. Nor is it a part of the evolutionary Law that the Fifth principle (Manas) should receive its complete development before the Fifth Round; prematurely developed intellects, (on the spiritual plane) in our Race are abnormal; they are those whom we have called the Fifth Rounders.

Even in the coming Seventh Race at the close of this Fourth Round, while our four lower principles will be fully developed, that of <u>Manas</u> will be only proportionately so. This limitation however refers solely to the spiritual development. The intellectual on the physical plane was reached during the Fourth Root Race, and those tribes of savages whose reasoning powers are very little above the level of animals, are not the <u>unjustly disinherited</u> or the unfavored; they are simply those latest arrivals among the human monads, and must evolve during the present Round, so also on the three remaining Globes, so as to arrive at the level of the average class when they reach the Fifth Round; but the savage South Sea Islander, the African, the Australian, had no Karma to work out when first born as men, as their more favored brethern in intelligence had; the former are only now spinning out their Karma. The latter are burdened with past, present and future Racial Karma. In this respect the poor savage is more fortunate than the greatest genius of civilized countries.

On the ascending Arc, Spirit is slowly reasserting itself at the expense of the physical or Matter; so that at the close of the Seventh Race the Monad will find itself as free from matter and all its qualities as it was in the beginning, having gained in addition the experience and Wisdom, the fruitage of all its personal lives without their evil and temptations.

This order of evolution is found in the first and second chapters of Genesis if one can read it in its esoteric sense. Chapter first contains the history of the first three Rounds as well as that of the first three Races; and the Fourth up to the moment when man is called to <u>Conscious Life</u> by the Elohim of Wisdom.

In Chapter First, animals, whales and fowls of the air are created before the Androgyne Adam (these are the sacred animals of the Zodiac); in Chapter Two, Adam (the sexless) comes first, and the real animals only appear after him.

The state of mental torpor and unconsciousness of the first two Races of the first half of the Third Race is symbolized by the <u>deep Sleep of Adam.</u> It is the dreamless sleep of mental inaction, the slumber of the Soul and Mind; and to this dreamless sleep we are going to return in the long sweep of time, or when time is no more. (This will be for rest).

In an important Greek manuscript we read - that the disciples say to Jesus, "Rabbi reveal unto us the mysteries of the Light (i.e., the Fire of Knowledge or Enlightenment) - for as much as we have heard the sayings that there is another baptism of smoke and another of the Spirit of Fire." John says of Jesus, "I indeed baptize you with water, but we shall baptize you with Fire." This means that John, a non-initiated ascetic, could impart to the disciples no greater wisdom than the mysteries connected with the plane of matter, of which water is the symbol.

In the cycle of initiation Water represents the first and lower steps toward purification, and trials connected with Fire come last. Water could regenerate the Body of Matter, Fire alone that of the Inner Spiritual Man. This is completion or all the end of time or the great seventh day of rest, when the Angel standing upon the Sea and upon the Earth lifted up his hand to Heaven and swore by him that liveth forever and ever that there should be times no longer, and when the voice of the second Angel shall begin to sound, the mystery of God, or the Cycle, should be finished. This means that when the Seventh Round is completed then time will cease, for there will remain no one on Earth to keep a division of time; Pralaya has come, a periodical dissolution and arrest of conscious Life.

Race after Race shall pass away as the ages roll on their course. New Continents will appear. Our great North America will in time be broken up by the earthquakes and subterranean fires; then Shaka will emerge from the waters to be the home of the Sixth Root Race. But as time moves on Shaka also shall pass away, overwhelmed by the mighty floods; then the mysterious Seventh Continent shall appear and flourish where South America is now to be found. Here on this marvelous Land called Pushkara, shall we find those people of the flower of evolution from Protoplasm back to God; that spiritual life baptised and regenerated by Fire. But this glorious Seventh Race also must pass away, and then will come the end of our Globe, its long eventful history will close, and it will sink peacefully to sleep after its eventful day of waking. For worlds pass away, Round succeeds Round, and Chain follows Chains, but the eternal spirit which is now clothed in human bodies remains and endureth forever.

Life after life in personal struggle passes by like the rank and file and rhythm of the marching multitude under the spell of a warrior's chant. We sow and we reap. We rise and we fall. We fill at times, important, and again inferior, gaps, and in the niches in the great Human Walls of various Races, learning that only the great Brotherhood of Humanity is worth while.

We weep and sometimes laugh, for we meet many sorrows and few joys along the El Camino Real of that weary journey called Life. But on and on we must continue our march toward Light, moved by the sway of Evolutionary Law, bearing on our own burdens, never seeking reward. But oh! How hard and fast beats the expectant heart in hope and thought of results. Shall we lose in that long and faithful struggle to reach the Goal, or shall we realize a triumphant entry into that Divine understanding which brings us the calm of sweet peace as we merged into the brilliant vibrating Light of the Eternal Majesty of all that is Universal Law.

Teach us O God, to pray - and KNOW.

THE LEGEND OF HIRAM ABIFF

Our lessons in this hall and elsewhere are designed to be an aid to those women who desire to comprehend some of the vast importance contained in the great truths of Masonry, and which are all concealed under a most incomprehensible and cunning symbology. The knowledge of this cult is scientific, philosophical and sublime. Its depth of meaning is the only religion of any value to the world. Its great mysteries, clothed in a wink and a smile by the common herds of the order, refer to the mighty problem of sex, the creative power, and procreation, typified by the God Jehovah of the Constantine Bible or masculine philosophy. These mysteries concern Woman more than Man, but were usurped or stolen from them in the far night of the past.

Knowledge that is good for man is also good for woman. But she, herself, must awaken to that fact. Knowledge cannot be imparted, it must be acquired. And to day we have a thankful heart for the noble women who compose our growing order. They are the pioneers in a work that will eventually be far reaching. One of the most important.

One of the most important allegories of Masonry is the legend of Hiram Abiff and belongs to the Third, or Master Mason's degree. We will endeavor in this lesson to give at least a small part of its meaning, hoping it may be understood. Bear in mind that many of the various initiations in the lodge symbolize the journey of Life upon this material plane, the gateway of which is typified by Jakin and Boaz, or man and woman, the Elohim of this plane. Gate or gateway in symbology typifies opportunity. Thus life here is an opportunity to gain something of a greater life, and intellectual rounding out of consciousness has been sadly limited for woman. And we find her at the present time, far behind in her proper and normal evolution, wandering in the tangled trails of the foothills, failing to even by able to look at light, confined in the darkest of ignorant environment, like the plant in the densely dark cellar, she has for centuries struggled toward the only feeble ray for her soul -- the Colossal Graft called Church, with its masculine horde of false teachers and selfish motives. The blind force leading the blind helplessness, until at the present time the ditch is overflowing with those who have fallen in. --- Teach us, O Great Divine Power, called God, to Watch, as well as to Pray. --- (Mark, 13,33).

We find the American Scottish Rite Ritual far superior in this phase of symbology than the Old English. Consequently we will use the best.

In the Third Master's Degree, after the candidate has taken the most barbarous oath, including not to be present at the initiation of an atheist, libertine, idiot, madman, hermaphrodite, WOMAN or fool, and that he will not violate the wife, mother, sister or daughter of a Master Mason, knowing them to be such, he is given his due guard sign, pass grip and word, Tubal Cain, also apron and working instruments, the trowel (significantly shaped). Then he is told of the three precious jewels, Humanity, Friendship, and Brotherly Love, after which is he thus addressed: "Brother, you are not yet invested with all

the secrets of this degree nor do I know whether you ever will be until I know
how you withstand the amazing trials and dangers that await you. You are now
about to travel to give us a specimen of your fortitude, perseverance and
fidelity in the preservation of that which has already been given you. Fare-
you-well, and may the Lord be with you as a support in all your trials and
difficulties. Let us in imitation of our Grand Master Hiram, kneel and pray
as follows: --

Thou, O God, knowest our down sitting and our uprising and understandest
our thoughts afar off. Shield us and defend us from the evil intentions of our
enemies, and support us under the trials and afflictions we are destined to en-
dure while traveling thru this vale of tears. Man, that is born of woman is of
few days and full of trouble. He cometh forth as a flower and is cut down.
He fleeth also as a shadow and continueth not. Seeing his days are determined,
the number of his months are with thee. Thou hast appointed his bounds that he
cannot pass, turn from him that he may rest until he shall accomplish his day.
For there is hope of a tree if it be cut down that it will sprout again and the
tender branch thereof will not cease. But man dieth and wasteth away. Yea,
man giveth the ghost and where is he? As the waters fail from the sea, and the
flood decayeth and drieth up, so man lieth down and riseth not up until the
heavens shall be no more. Let, O, Lord, have compassion on the children of thy
creation. Administer unto them, comfort in the time of trouble, and save them
with an everlasting salvation. Amen. "So mote it be."

The candidate and conductor now rise, and the conductor says: "Brother,
in further imitation of our Grand Master Hiram Abiff, let us retire to the
South Gate." The room is dark or otherwise the candidate is hood-winked, symbolizing the ignorance of the unawakened. Hiram or Kheureum, is the Christ-
principle or Firemist body on its journey back to the home of Intelligent Fire
and Light. The South Gate is the place of Spiritual instability. In other
words, our early days of ignorance in the school of Life. At this Gate the
candidate meets the assassin of falsity called Jubela. The Hebrew word, Jubel
(or Guibel) means limit, boundary - supposed in this case to refer to the lim-
itations of spirit matter. The last letter "A" is the first letter in the sacred syllable A U M, and stands for Angi or Fire. The assassin of falsehood,
Jubela, at the South Gate strikes the candidate who represents the Grand Master
Hiram Abiff, across the throat with a 24 inch guage. After seizing him roughly
by the throat and jerking him about demanding the word of the Master Mason.
This might impress one as "horse play" and the vast majority of the Masonic
Body, who are hurriedly rushed thru the various stages of the degree, could
comprehend in this seeming farce nothing better. But let us now examine its
symbolic meaning.

First we have the number 24 as a measure. Two means the multitude. Four
means the plane of natural life at the Southern Gate. The name Jubela (junior
warden), the limitation of the Firemist in matter. The candidate is struck across the throat...the organs of speech seeking for truth or light in the darkness or ignorance of the true knowledge of the journey of life. Now let us read
that the multitudes in the spiritual instability of natural life are seriously
injured by false speech, misled from the great knowledge of Fire worship by
false religions that have for centuries festered and fed hatred, graft, cunning
and ignorance, have produced more war bloodshed and destruction than any other

-47-

common source of evil, inventing all the inconceivable implements of human torture to subjugate and control the intellect, and dominate the judgement of the vast moving multitude, all in the name of the Prince of Characters who says "A new commandment give I unto you, that ye Love One another." Under these wrongs and injustice, Woman has ever been the easiest victim, as we shall observe in the following.

The candidate was injured by the assassin Jubela and flies to the Western Gate. This Gate symbolizes the greatest evil, or alienation from God. Here is met the assassin Jubelo or Jubelu. Both O and U signify Woman or man's tendency on this plane. This ruffian seizes the candidate violently (also demanding the Word, which is always refused). He is then struck across the breast with the square - separated from the compass - which also symbolizes Woman and material life. The blow staggers him but he does not fall.

This deadly assailant signifies superstition. The breast is the home of the heart and the seat of the emotions. When superstition rules, the emotions will ever triumph over reason and judgement which is a staggering blow. This most objectionable phase of character is festered and fed in woman by the agonizing fables of the Church, vividly portrayed by masculine orators, who in the majority are Masons and sufficiently enlightened to understand the benighting effect, but fail to give public recognition of that fact that what chains woman is benighted ignorance - also enslaves the equal to sustain the temple here and to build the mansions of light beyond. The chance should be equal in the march of light.

The candidate now attempts to make his escape at the Eastern Gate. This Gate typifies the source of light --- the nearest approach of God. Here is met the most formidable assassin of all: Jubelum (Worshipful Master). O is feminine, M is androgynous. On the candidate's refusal to comply with the request he strikes the candidate a violent blow on the forehead with the gavel and fells him to the floor. This assassin represents ignorance. The common gavel of the lodge signifies power, force; and thus the force and power of the terrible assailant ignorance, fells us all as a multitude, to the threshing floor of Oman, the Jebusite. There to struggle as best we can with no knowledge of the mighty laws of life, which are ever merciless, pitiless, and compassionless to the ignorant, under the grind of the mill-stones.

The assassins now say "We have killed our Grand Master, Hiram Abiff (the Divine Consciousness is destroyed by falsehood, superstition and ignorance). Let us carry him out at the East Gate (on another plane) and bury him in the rubbish (which means that which is cast off, or cannot remain). We will leave him there until low twelve, then meet and carry him a westerly course and bury him." Low twelve is midnight -- darkness -- the density of ignorance which forces the soul-consciousness back on this plane at the Westerly direction -- the greatest alienation of Light -- to be again buried or reincarnated in the great human life wave.

Now let us consider this far-reaching symbology. In the names of the assassins we find the sacred monosyllable A.U.M. and he who does not know A.U.M. passes out of life in dense ignorance. He also knows the supreme essence of all Bibles, for it contains a meaning as old as the world, and better under-

will observe in this journey of the candidate he could not give the Word, or the important concealed lost knowledge, to either of the assassins who demanded it. Neither can it be given today to a world of humanity overflowing with falsity, superstition and ignorance, combined with all their train of evils including treachery, maliciousness, greed, selfishness, cunning and crime. But let us ask, would humanity have thus developed if the truth had been kept before them? Instead of being stolen, crucified, and concealed by selfish magicians who so cheerfully substituted falsity, superstition and ignorance? Enthroning it under gilt, tinsel and gew-gaws to attract the gaze of the multitude from the Real to the Unreal, Saying "Look and believe!" And the great mass of humanity are still looking and paying a salary for the privilege.

The knowledge of Life is contained in the sacred A.U.M. - A or Angi, means Fire; U or Usuas, means the Dawn. The first is masculine, the second feminine in dominance; but each contains the Potencies of both. M or Mitka is the transcendent, glowing wisdom of the Sun, or the Supreme Androgynous state of Agni and Ushas (Fire - masculine; Light - Feminine; ...Mitra). In the six syllables of these sacred letters we have Indragni or Light and Spiritual Wisdom. Then Venus Urania, or Heavenly Love. Again A.U.M. symbolizes the Great Divine Invisible Triangle of which the small illumined triangle in the lodge is a visible correspondence. And the chanting of the name as a mantram upon the keynote of M is the cry of the struggling and imprisoned soul for recognition. "I am in Thee and Thou in Me, O Divine Creative Power." And A.U.M. Signifies the bonded indissoluble union between the souls of mankind and the great supreme intelligent essence of that Cosmic Power called God. One of the greatest of Masons was never a Mason only as the Divine within him triumphed over the human in his march toward Light.

A.U.M. signifies both the Divine and the Light. And he who knows A.U.M. knows Hiram and the legend also the Vedas and all Bibles. "Thou Great Eternal Infinite!" Thou Great Unbounded Whole! Thy Body is the Universe -- Thy Spirit is its Soul! If thou dost fill immensity --- If Thou art All in All I am in Thee and Thou in me -- or I'm not here at all. How can I be outside of Thee when Thou fill earth and air, There surely is no place for me outside of everywhere. Then truly, in Thyself and I, and Thou must be in me -- else there is no All in All -- nor me -- nor Thee -- to Be.

The true legend of Hiram is that falsehood, superstition and ignorance have destroyed the Truth. We observe the fatal blow was struck by Jubelum, thus we learn that Ignorance of the Great Law of the letters U. and M. is the most fatal condition for us to exist in both here and hereafter. The names of the three wicked assassins are mere inventions to conceal this sacred word, until it could be restored in the place of the substitutes. But a careful study of the substitute word reveals it most ingeniously concealed. This A.U.M. is as old as the world and its secret lies in exact vibrations. Its Law is equilibrium and eternal harmony. It has existed among all the ancient peoples of the earth. It is the Amen of Orthodoxy, and was at one time found and understood in the Master Mason's degree.

All masonry is contained in the symbology of the Blue Lodge or first three degrees. Blue means under the Law. It reads the Lodge under the Law and four degrees should be the limit of all understanding. Graft and selfish cunning have made degrees unlimited. "Forever and forever whatsoever a man soweth, that also shall he reap." It may be only in the long sweep of time, but "Vengeance is mine. "I will repay, Saith the Law."

H. P. Blavatsky

AN OUTLINE OF HER LIFE.

BY

HERBERT WHYTE,

WITH A PREFACE BY

C. W. LEADBEATER.

LONDON

THE LOTUS JOURNAL, 42, Craven Road, Paddington, W.

CITY:

H. P. BLAVATSKY.

CONTENTS.

FOREWORD.

This brief outline of the life of Madame Blavatsky, co-founder with Colonel Olcott of the Theosophical Society, appeared in serial form in the *Lotus Journal*. It was written with the hope that a fuller acquaintance with the life of the Light-bringer might still further endear her to those to whom she brought the Light.

I have to acknowledge my great indebtedness to *Incidents in the Life of Madame Blavatsky*, by A. P. Sinnett, *Old Diary Leaves*, by H. S. Olcott, and *Reminiscences of H. P. B.* by Countess Wachtmeister.

H. W.

PREFACE.

The very first news that I ever heard of our great Founder, Madame Blavatsky, was curious and characteristic, and the hearing of it was a most important event in my life, though I did not know it then. A staunch friend of my school days took up the sea-life as his profession, and about the year 1879 he was second officer on board one of the coasting vessels of the British India Steam Navigation Co. On her voyage from Bombay to Colombo Madame Blavatsky happened to travel by that steamer, and thus my friend was brought into contact with that marvellous personality.

He told me two very curious stories about her. It seems that one evening he was on deck trying vainly to light a pipe in a high wind. Being on duty he could not leave the deck, so he struck match after match only to see the flame instantly extinguished by the gale. Finally, with an expression of impatience, he abandoned the attempt. As he straightened himself he saw just below him a dark form closely wrapped in a cloak, and Madame Blavatsky's clear voice called to him :

" Cannot you light it, then ? "

" No," he replied, " I do not believe that anyone could keep a match alight in such a wind as this."

" Try once more," said Madame Blavatsky.

He laughed, but he struck another match, and he assures me that, in the midst of that gale and quite unprotected from it, that match burnt with a steady flame clear down to the fingers that held it. He was so astounded that he quite forgot to light his pipe after all, but H.P.B. only laughed and turned away.

On another occasion during the voyage the first officer made, in Madame Blavatsky's presence, some casual reference to what he would do on the return voyage from Calcutta. (The steamers go round the coast from Bombay to Calcutta and back again). She interrupted him, saying :

" No, you will not do that, for you will not make the return voyage at all. When you reach Calcutta you will be appointed captain of another steamer, and you will go in quite a different direction."

" Madam," said the first officer, " I wish with all my heart you might be right, but it is impossible. It is true I hold a captain's certificate, but there are many before me on the list for promotion. Besides, I have signed an agreement to serve on this coasting run for five years."

" All that does not matter," replied Madame Blavatsky ; " you will find it will all happen as I tell you."

And *it did* ; for when that steamer reached Calcutta it was found that an unexpected vacancy had occurred (I think through the sudden death of a captain), and there was no one at hand who could fill it but that same first officer. So the prophecy which had seemed so impossible was literally fulfilled.

These were points of no great importance in themselves, but they implied a great deal, and their influence on me was in an indirect manner very great. For in less than a year after that conversation Mr. Sinnett's book, *The Occult World*, fell into my hands, and as soon as I saw Madame Blavatsky's name mentioned in it I at once recalled the stories related to me by my earliest friend. Naturally the strong first-hand evidence which I had already had of her phenomenal powers predisposed me to admit the possibility of these other strange new things of which Mr. Sinnett wrote, and thus those two little stories played no unimportant part in my life, since they prepared me for the instant and eager acceptance of theosophical truth.

It was in 1884 that I first had the privilege of meeting Madame Blavatsky, and before the end of that year I was travelling from Egypt to India with her in the s.s. *Navarino*. The training through which she put her pupils was somewhat severe, but remarkably effective ; I can testify to certain radical changes which her drastic methods produced in *me* in a very short space of time—also to the fact that they have been permanent !

I think I ought also to bear witness to the genuineness of those phenomena about which such a storm of controversy has raged. I had the opportunity of seeing several such happenings under circumstances which rendered any theory of fraud absolutely untenable, even at that time, when I did not in the least understand how such things could be. Now, as the result of later study, I know the methods which she must have employed, and what was then so incomprehensible appears perfectly simple.

If I were asked to mention Madame Blavatsky's most prominent characteristic, I should unhesitatingly reply " Power." Apart from the great Masters of Wisdom, I have never known any person from whom power so visibly radiated. Any man who was introduced to her at once felt himself in the presence of a tremendous force—to which he was quite unaccustomed; he realized with disconcerting vividness that those wonderful pale blue eyes saw clearly through him, and not infrequently she would soon drop some casual remark which proved to him that his apprehensions in that regard were well founded. Some people did not like to find themselves thus unexpectedly transparent, and for that reason they cordially hated Madame Blavatsky, while others loved—and love—her with whole-hearted devotion, knowing well how much they owe her and how great is the work which she has done. So forceful was she that no one ever felt indifferent towards her ; every one experienced either strong attraction or strong repulsion.

Clever she certainly was. Not a scholar in the ordinary sense of the word, yet possessed of apparently inexhaustible stores of unusual knowledge on all sorts of out-of-the-way unexpected subjects. Witty, quick at repartee, a most brilliant conversationalist, and a dramatic *raconteuse* of the weirdest stories I have ever heard—many of them her own personal experiences. She was an indefatigable worker from early in the morning until late at night, and she expected everyone around her to share her enthusiasm and her marvellous endurance. She was always ready to sacrifice herself —and, for the matter of that, others also—for the sake of the cause, of the great work upon which she was engaged. Utter devotion to her Master and to His work was the dominant note of her life, and though now she wears a different body that note still sounds out unchanged, and when she comes forth from her retirement to take charge once more of the Society which she founded, we shall find it ringing in our ears as a clarion to call round her old friends and new, so that through all the ages that work shall still go on.

It is well, indeed, that our members should know something of the last life of their Founder, and so this little book, gathering together as it does the outlines of that life from sources not accessible to the majority, fills a vacant place in our library, and meets a real need. May it meet with the success which it deserves ; may it, by leading us better to understand and appreciate one messenger from the Great White Lodge, inspire us with comprehension of and loyalty to its present Representative, and thus be a link in the golden chain of love and mutual understanding which binds us all together.

C. W. LEADBEATER.

H. P. BLAVATSKY.

CHAPTER I.

CHILDHOOD, 1831-1844.*

The powerful, strongly-marked face of the co-founder of the Theosophical Society must be familiar to many, as her portrait is to be found in most of the Society's meeting-rooms, and has been printed in many places. But how few know the story of her arduous life? No one knows it fully, nor is it anywhere completely recorded, save in the imperishable memory of nature, wherein the history of every life is preserved. Several books have, however, been written about Madame Blavatsky, and from them the following outline of her life is compiled.

Helena Petrovna Hahn was born at Ekaterinoslow in the South of Russia, in 1831. Her father, Col. Hahn, was an officer in the Russian army, who belonged to a noble family coming from Mecklenburg, Germany, and her mother, Helene Fadeef, who attained some fame as an authoress, was the daughter of Princess Dolgorouky, and so came of one of the oldest Russian aristocratic families.

The baby, whose career has meant so much to many of us, was born in the night between July 30th and 31st—a feeble little infant which was not expected to

* Compiled from *Incidents in the Life of Mdme. Blavatsky*, A. P. Sinnett.

live. They decided that it must be baptised at once, and so all the preparations were made for this important ceremony; a large room was selected and the whole household assembled, everyone being provided with a burning taper which had to be held during the service. A little girl, the child-aunt of the baby, who was in the front row, grew very tired, and settled, unobserved, on the floor with her lighted taper in her hand; the sponsors were just in the act of renouncing the Evil One and his deeds, when they discovered that the long flowing robes of the priest had caught fire from the little girl's taper, and the poor old man was rather severely burnt. This was considered by the superstitious servants to be a bad omen, and a troubled and eventful life was predicted for poor little Helena Hahn.

Contrary to expectations the baby lived and grew up, although for some years her health was delicate; but it improved greatly, for at ten years of age she was a good rider, and at fifteen she could control any Cossack horse; a Cossack horse is generally considered to have a will and a way of its own, but so had Helena Hahn. She was daring, very lively, and full of humour, with a passionate love for everything unknown and mysterious, and a craving for independence and freedom of action.

The child's nurses were familiar with, and fully believed in all the legends and customs relating to the fairies and the goblins, and they were persuaded that Helena had some touch with the unseen worlds; 'thus on a certain day in July, each year, her nurse would carry her all round the establishment, and make her sprinkle the four corners with water, the nurse repeat-

1848

ing mystic sentences the while. Sometimes, when she was older and understood her superiority better, little Helena would frighten the poor nurse by telling her about these goblins, and so gain her own way when the nurse wished otherwise. For two or three years Helena and her younger sister went to stay with their father, and moved about with the soldiers of whom he had command ; they were chiefly taken care of by their father's orderlies, and Helena, at least, greatly preferred them to her female nurses.

Before Helena was eleven her mother died and she was taken to live with her grandmother, Princess Dolgorouky, at Saratow, where she spent five years. The house was an old rambling castle-like place, with subterranean passages and weird nooks and corners ; and there was a large park which joined on to the deep forest, full of shadows and sombre paths. Many legends were related about the old place, which Helena quickly learnt. Altogether it was a home that was likely still further to quicken that love of the mysterious which was already so strong a trait in her character. She was a highly-strung, sensitive girl, given to walking in her sleep, sometimes full of mischief, and at other times as assiduous at her lessons as an old scholar. For her all nature seemed animated with a mysterious life of its own ; she heard the voice of every object and form ; she talked with birds and animals, and had some means of her own for understanding them, while inanimate objects, such as certain stuffed specimens of seals and crocodiles, and old antediluvian monsters which the house contained, suggested endless romances to her lively imagination. Sometimes

B

they were more than fancies which she wove round these objects, and often she would relate her stories to a group of younger children ; seated on her favourite animal, a huge stuffed seal, she would repeat his adventures, as told her by himself, or tell the romance of a tall white flamingo, whose behaviour while alive had left something to be desired, so that all the younger children grew quite afraid of him, even though he was stuffed. Her power of story-telling was remarkable, for she seemed actually to live in the events she was describing, and quite carried her audience away with her.

She made the acquaintance of an old man, a centenarian, who was popularly considered to be a wizard, but of a benevolent type, for he willingly cured those who applied to him in sickness, using herbs whose properties he well knew. He kept bees, and in the summer could be seen walking among his favourites and *covered* by them from head to foot, as by a living cloak, while he could put his hands into their hives with impunity ; the buzzing of the bees would stop when he spoke in a curious way to them—evidently he and they understood one another. Helena visited this strange old man whenever possible, and listened with eager interest to all he had to say about the language of the birds and beasts.

Besides these unusual elements which were added to the ordinary events of her childhood, there was another influence of great importance which ought to be mentioned. At a very early period of her life Helena was aware of a Protector, invisible to all but herself, a man of imposing appearance, whose features never changed, and whom she met in after life as a living man, and knew as though she had been brought up in his presence. This guardianship never forsook her throughout her life, as we shall see, and it showed itself even in her childhood as the following stories will show.

When she was about fourteen a horse bolted with her ; she fell with her foot entangled in the stirrup, and before the horse was stopped she ought to have been killed outright but for a strange sustaining power, which she distinctly felt around her and which seemed to hold her up in defiance of gravitation.

When she was quite a small mite another surprising adventure befell her. She conceived a wish to inspect closely a picture which hung high on a wall with a curtain in front of it—a wish which was not responded to by her elders. So when the coast was clear, determined to carry out her design, she dragged a table to the wall, and contriving to place another small table upon that, and a chair on the top of all, she succeeded in mounting this unstable erection, and found she could just reach the picture by leaning with one hand on the dusty wall, while with the other she pulled back the curtain. The picture startled her, her slight movement upset her frail platform and . . . exactly what occurred she could not say. But she lost consciousness from the moment she began to fall, and when she recovered her senses was lying quite unhurt on the floor, the tables and chairs were in their usual places, the curtain was in front of the picture, and the only sign of her adventure was the mark of her small hand on the dusty wall high up beside the picture.

There was one trait in our heroine's character which showed itself in her early youth, and remained with her all through her life, and that was her sympathy for those who were of a humbler station in life than herself. As a child, she always preferred to play with the servants' children rather than with her equals, and had constantly to be watched lest she should escape from the house and make friends with ragged street boys. So, later in life, she cared nothing for mere nobility of birth, and always was especially sympathetic towards those who were socially beneath her.

CHAPTER II.

GIRLHOOD. 1844-1853.

In 1844 Colonel Hahn took Helena to Paris and to London, one of the objects of the journey being to obtain for her some good music lessons, as she showed great natural abilities as a pianist—abilities which never altogether forsook her during later life, although they sometimes found no opportunity of expression for years together. The visit was not altogether a success, partly owing to our heroine's peculiarities of temperament and she was disappointed to find that her knowledge of English was more imperfect that she had realized. She had learned from an English governess who hailed from Yorkshire and who had taught the English language with the broad o's and a's which distinguish the Yorkshire version of it, so that Mdlle. Hahn's combination of Yorkshire and South Russian raised smiles among her English friends which she herself did not deem warranted by the substance of her remarks. It should be added, however, that before her next visit to England some years later, this defect had been remedied and the Russian linguistic ability had asserted itself, so that she spoke English well.

The marriage, in 1848, which transformed Mademoiselle Helena Hahn into Madame Blavatsky, came about in a somewhat curious way. She was an eagle in a nest of sparrows, and, as we have seen, her difference of character had already appeared. She was

" dared " by her governess to find any man who would be her husband, and she accepted the challenge. General Blavatsky, the governor of a Russian province, was quite an elderly man, of whom she had by no means a lofty opinion, but in three days' time she made him propose to her. Too late, she discovered that her joking acceptance was really a serious matter and that she would have to face all the consequences. The whole thing was nothing more than a girlish prank—she was only seventeen at the time—and perhaps its results were not much greater than those involved in the mere change of name. Her friends tried to impress upon her the solemnity of the step which she was about to take ; her one desire was to break off the engagement so rashly made, but this was not listened to, and on the appointed day the marriage took place.

Before three months had passed the young bride resolved to leave her husband ; she took horse and rode away from the country house in which they were spending the orthodox honeymoon. After some family counsels she set out to join her father, who had been far away in Russia with his regiment during the foregoing events, but during the journey she began to fear that Col. Hahn might insist upon her returning to General Blavatsky, so she decided to take the law into her own hands again and to give her escort—an old serving-man and a maid—the slip. Part of their journey was by ship to a place called Kertch ; on reaching this port she sent the servants ashore to find apartments and prepare them for her. Then by a liberal outlay of roubles she persuaded the captain to sail away for his next port ! It was an adventurous voyage for a girl of eighteen, for at the next port, in order to escape the harbour police, she had to borrow the outfit of the cabin boy, who hid in the coal bunker ! At Constantinople, however, she had the good fortune to meet a Russian lady of her acquaintance, with whom she safely travelled for some time. No complete record of these European travels exist ; it appears that she visited Cairo, where she met an old man who had considerable reputation as a magician, from whom she received some instruction ; and in Paris she formed the acquaintance of a famous mesmerist, who discovered her wonderful psychic gifts and was eager to retain her as one of his sensitives. This was by no means to Madame's liking, and in order to escape his influence she quitted Paris hastily.

At about this time she paid her second visit to London, during which an important event occurred which Countess Wachtmeister relates.* We have already heard that, from her early childhood, our heroine was conscious of a guiding and guarding Presence, very dignified, very benignant, unseen to any save herself. She had learnt to think of this Presence as her Guardian and to feel that she was under His protection. One day, when she was out walking she saw a tall Hindu with some Indian princes. To her astonishment she recognised in him the Guardian whom she had already come to revere. Her first impulse was to rush forward and speak to him, but he made her a sign not to move, and she stood as if spell-bound while he passed by. The next day she went

---

* *Reminiscences of H. P. Blavatsky*, p. 56.

to Hyde Park for a stroll, that she might be alone and free to think over her extraordinary adventure. Looking up she saw the same dignified Hindu approaching her, this time with the purpose of meeting her and speaking to her. He explained that he had come to London with the Indian princes on an important mission, and that he was desirous of meeting her physically, as he wished to have her co-operation in a work which he was about to undertake. He then gave her some information as to the work she would be called upon to perform and told her that she would have many troubles and difficulties to face and also that she would have to spend three years in Thibet to prepare her for her work.

We have no written record of the impression this interview made upon the mind of our young heroine, but it is not difficult to realize that the meeting in the physical body with that Guardian whom she already knew in an interior way, and the counsel which she then received, must have had far-reaching consequences in her life. One is reminded of a rather similar occurrence in the life of another mystic—Jacob Böhme. A mysterious customer came one day when Jacob, then a lad, was alone in the shoe-maker's shop where he was serving his apprenticeship ; poor Jacob transacted the business as best he could and then the stranger called him out and, taking him by the hand, told him briefly that he had great work to do in the world, and gave him good advice as to how he should prepare himself for it.

But the time for Madame Blavatsky's great work in the world was still far ahead and her intense love of adventure and dislike for any constraint were very strong. Her fancy led her to America in pursuit of North American Indians as she imagined them to be, after reading Fennimore Cooper's delightful stories. She was introduced to a party of Indians in some Canadian city and forthwith settled down for a long conference with them about their customs and the doings of their medicine men. Apparently she found the talk of their doings in the forest and wigwam so absorbing that their doings in her room escaped her observation ; they departed, and with them certain of Madame Blavatsky's belongings ! Disappointed in her hopes of the sons and daughters of the Wild West she made her way to New Orleans, where the strange magical rites practised by a sect of West African negroes, known as Voodoos, excited her curiosity. These rites, however, were of a very un-desirable character, and so she moved on to pastures new.

Mexico provided her with interesting material and also with the necessary number of adventures, without which no single year of her life was complete. It is wonderful that she passed unscathed through all these wanderings ; nothing stood her in such good stead as the magic of her own fearlessness. During these Mexican wanderings she resolved to go to India to try to meet again that Teacher whom she now knew physically. Strange as it may seem, she had already met two others who were bent on a similar quest ; one an Englishman and the other a Hindu. The three pilgrims, presumably in 1852, but that date is not certain, reached Bombay, where their paths separated. Madame Blavatsky did not succeed in her quest on this first occasion, only getting as far as Nepal, where she was compelled to turn back. She returned to England in 1853, but the preparations for the Crimean War offended her patriotic feelings, and she crossed to America, going this time to New York, and afterwards to the Far West and across the Rocky Mountains with emigrants' caravans, till she reached San Francisco, where she stayed for some time.

CHAPTER III.

ADVENTURES AND WONDERS.
1855-1867.

After waiting for two years in America, Madame Blavatsky again set out for the "burnished and mysterious East," which ever attracted her so strongly, and reached Calcutta in 1855. That she was able to travel about in this way was due to her father, with whom she kept in touch, and who provided her with the necessary funds at convenient opportunities; her other relatives never heard from her, as she wished to run no risks of being taken back to the household life in Russia, from which, as we have seen, she had cut herself free. As I have before remarked, it is as useless to look for a conformity to the ordinary conventions of life in *this* biography as to expect the career of an eagle to conform to the views of life held by a sparrow. With three companions Madame journeyed through Kashmir, under the guidance of a Tartar Shaman or monk; these men are often quite illiterate, but are sometimes well versed in certain forms of practical magic. Their aim was to penetrate into Tibet, but they had only proceeded sixteen miles, when two of them were politely escorted back to the frontier, while the third would-be explorer was stricken down with fever and had to return to India. Our heroine persevered, however, and invested with an appropriate disguise by the Shaman, pushed far into the " Forbidden Land."

Like the Abbé Huc, who was one of the earliest travellers to record his recollections of these little-known lands, Madame Blavatsky saw many strange things, and her interest in all forms of magic was amply gratified. Her friend, the Shaman, constantly carried a stone talisman under his arm which excited her curiosity, and in answer to her questions would only promise to explain when a convenient opportunity offered. One day when a certain ceremony had called all the people of the village away, Madame Blavatsky repeated her question about the talisman. The Shaman agreed to explain, but first he fixed up a goat's-head at the entrance of the tent as a warning to the villagers that he was not to be disturbed. He then settled himself down and proceeded, as it seemed, to *swallow the stone*. Almost immediately he fell into a deep swoon and his body became rigid and cold. Here was a worthy situation for our adventure-loving heroine; in a tent in mid-Mongolia, with the sun sinking rapidly in the West, and the profoundest silence enveloping all—her sole companion an apparently lifeless Shaman. Is it any wonder that her thoughts turned to Russia and her friends? Presently, however, a deep voice spoke through the cold lips of her companion, asking what she would have. Madame was fairly collected, having seen such trances before and knowing something of their nature and possibilities. She therefore demanded that the invisible questioner who spoke through the body before her, should visit three of her friends. First she sent him to an old friend, a Roumanian lady of a somewhat mystic temperament, who was described as sitting in her garden reading a letter, which was dictated slowly to Madame Blavatsky, who wrote it down. Then in a corner of the tent the misty form of this old lady appeared for a few minutes. Months afterwards it was ascertained that on that very day and hour the old lady had been quietly sitting in the garden reading a letter from her brother ; it was this letter which the Shaman dictated to Madame Blavatsky. Suddenly the old lady fainted and remembered dreaming that she " saw Helen in a deserted place, under a gypsy's tent." For two hours the astral body of the entranced Shaman travelled at Madame's bidding, reporting to her as to far distant friends and places. In particular she directed him to a friend possessed also of occult powers, asking for means of return to more civilised parts ; a few hours later a party of twenty-five horsemen rode up and rescued her from the perilous situation in which she had involved herself.

After relating this adventure (see *Isis Unveiled*) Madame Blavatsky adds that while some may disbelieve her statements others will see in them an interesting instance of the powers of the human soul when freed from the body as the Shaman was. He, of course, was only a medium, not a veritable adept. The story is also interesting as showing the invariable respect which Madame commanded among those who possessed partial control of some of the finer forces of Nature.

This incident put an end for the time being to her wanderings in Tibet ; she was conducted back to the frontier and after some further travels in India was directed by her occult guardian to leave the country, shortly before the Mutiny which broke out in 1857.

Her family in Russia had heard nothing of her except the vaguest rumours ; it was Christmas night, 1858, a wedding-party was in progress, when in the midst of the supper an impatient ring at the bell was heard, and Madame Blavatsky walked in !

At the time of which we write (1858) Madame Blavatsky was already possesesd of occult powers, and the next few years of her life, spent in Russia with her family, were crowded with marvellous occurrences, of which she was the central figure. Mysterious raps and whisperings were constantly heard in her presence, while occasionally the most astonishing things happened. The phenomona which surrounded her were similar to those sometimes found among mediums, but, unlike the latter, Madame Blavatsky had these manifestations to a great extent under her control, and this power to control and if necessary to stop them, was one which grew stronger. She considered *mediumship*, which consists essentially in the surrender of that control, which we usually exercise, over the physical and etheric bodies in favour of some other entity or entities, to be degrading to human dignity. The following story is typical of many of the occurrences which happened at this time. Madame Blavatsky was in the drawing-room with her relatives, many of whom were sceptical as to her powers. Her brother, who believed in no one and nothing, was expressing his disbelief somewhat frankly, when Madame Blavatsky declared that she would so fix a small chess table to the floor *without touching it* that it could not be lifted. Her friends gathered eagerly round her while she fixed her eyes, with an intense gaze, upon the little table. Then, with a motion of her hand she directed one of the young men present to lift it. He stooped confidently down and seized it by the leg, but—the table was immovable, as though screwed to the floor. He was a muscular youth and disinclined to be beaten, so exerting all his strength and using his broad shoulders, he tried again, but in vain. The table seemed to be *rooted to the spot.* Her brother now stepped forward and met with no more success, although he gave the diminutive table a tremendous kick. Seeing the astonishment on the faces of all present Madame Blavatsky, with a laugh said, " Try once more." Her brother very irresolutely approached the bewitched table ; grasping it by the leg, however, he gave it a good heave up and nearly dislocated his arm owing to the useless effort, for the table was lifted like a feather this time !

Her father, Colonel Hahn, was utterly sceptical as to his daughter's marvellous powers, at which he simply laughed. One day, however, two old friends of his who had just convinced themselves absolutely of the genuineness of her psychic gifts, persuaded him to devise a test himself. The old gentleman, probably hoping to have a good laugh at their expense, proceeded into the next room and wrote a word on a slip of paper, which he folded and put in his pocket ; he then returned to his game of *Patience,* quietly smiling behind his gray moustache. All the others present gathered expectantly round, while the familiar raps were heard on a plate ; a young lady repeated the alphabet and at the proper letter a rap was made; Madame Blavatsky did nothing at all—apparently. Slowly, letter by letter, a word was written down— a queer word, which so puzzled them all that they felt sure there must be some mistake. " Well, what have you got ? " called out Colonel Hahn. " One word—' *Zaïtchik*.' " The old gentleman's face was a study ! With a trembling hand he examined the paper, muttering, " How very strange." Then pulling out his folded paper he handed it to them in silence. It bore the same word—the name of his favourite war horse in the Turkish war years ago ! From that day Colonel Hahn was firmly convinced of his daughter's gifts and studied them closely ; he sought her aid in completing a history of his family, and marvelled at the completeness and accuracy with which she was able to give him, by means of her psychic powers, all the details he wanted.

Well, these are merely specimens of many wonderful tales for which readers are referred to *Incidents in the Life of Madame Blavatsky*, by Mr. Sinnett. As might be expected, the report of all these strange happenings got abroad, and Madame Blavatsky soon came to be regarded as a magician. About this time, however, she was taken seriously ill, and for days she lay like one apparently dead. She recovered, but from that time every phenomenon independent of her will entirely ceased. In her case, as in so many others, a serious illness has marked an important change in the life. The struggle of her earlier years was to obtain control over the mysterious forces of the inner side of nature which were always playing around her, and her victory seems to have coincided with this serious illness.

1870.

CHAPTER IV.

FROM APPRENTICESHIP TO DUTY.
1867-1875.

The period of her life from 1867-70, if it could be told, would probably prove of great interest. But all that is known of these years is that they were spent in the East, and that a great increase in occult knowledge was their fruit. They mark the transition from " apprenticeship to duty " as Mr. Sinnett puts it, for Madame Blavatsky returned from the East with much of the knowledge which it was her great but enormously difficult task to re-introduce to the world.

It requires but a slight exercise of the imagination to realize something of the task which lay before Madame Blavatsky. The work of introducing to a world either entirely ignorant of, or greatly prejudiced against, the Eastern teachings which we now term Theosophy, was one which only the bravest heart and the most devoted character could carry through ; but our heroine possessed these two qualities in a splendid degree. She was a Russian, and, for the most part, had to speak and write in languages that were not her own ; her teachings were new and strange, and utterly opposed to many of the religious views then prevailing ; not only had she to face opposition, but also she had the great initial difficulty of finding out how and when to start. There was no Theosophical

c

Society with its own Publishing Department waiting to receive and propagate her teachings ! She had to find the people scattered through the world who were likely to appreciate and understand her. Although Madame Blavatsky was a pupil of one of the Great Masters and was entrusted with this piece of work, we must not suppose that the precise details and methods of action were given to her ; nor do we find that she herself fully understood, at first, all the teaching which later she was to give out so abundantly.

In 1870 she returned from the East, meeting with her customary adventures *en route*, for a dreadful explosion occurred on her ship, and she was among the very few on board who were picked out of the water. She managed to reach Cairo, where she suffered many inconveniences until money reached her from Russia. In Cairo, she found a certain number of people who were interested in Spiritualism, and concluded that it would be wise to start work among them. She hoped to show them that she herself could produce at will the phenomena which ordinarily they obtained through a medium, and thereby to awaken their interest in the deeper side of her teachings. But her efforts met with no success, as a number of quite unsuitable people attached themselves to her and speedily brought the little society into such disrepute that Madame Blavatsky severed her connection with it, although she had already given some important demonstrations of her own powers.

She again met the venerable Copt, of whom we have already spoken, and saw many of the wonders of Egypt ; in particular she passed a night in the black darkness of the King's Chamber in the Great Pyramid, comfortably settled in a sarcophagus ! A characteristic recreation ! One other acquaintance she made at this time who ought to be mentioned, *viz.*, Madame Coulomb, then attached to a small hotel in Cairo ; years afterwards this person and her husband, finding themselves in great destitution in India, availed themselves of Madame Blavatsky's generous help and repaid her kindness by an act of cruel ingratitude, as we shall see later on. At the end of 1872 her family at Odessa were surprised by Madame Blavatsky's unannounced return, but the bird of passage did not settle for long. In 1873 she started on her travels again, this time turning Westward for the soil in which she might plant the seeds of Eastern thought with which she was entrusted.

An incident which occurred on this journey was so characteristic of her and so similar to many others which are remembered by those who knew Madame Blavatsky, that it is well to record it here. Madame Blavatsky had taken a first-class ticket for New York, and was going on board the steamer at Havre, when she saw a poor woman with two little children, standing on the pier and weeping bitterly. " Why are you crying ? " she asked. The woman replied that her husband had sent to her, from America, money to enable her and her children to join him. She had expended it all in the purchase, from a bogus Steamship Agent, of steerage tickets which turned out to be fraudulent imitations. She could not find the rogue who sold them to her, and was quite penniless in a strange city. Madame Blavatsky went to the Agent of the Steamship Company and induced him to exchange her own first-class ticket for steerage tickets for herself, the poor woman and the children. Thus it happened that our heroine travelled to America in the crowded discomfort of the steerage of a liner.

At the time of her arrival at New York (1873) a series of remarkable spiritualistic phenomena were commencing to attract much attention. William and Horatio Eddy were farmers at Chittenden, Vermont, U.S.A. ; they were poor and ill-educated, but strong mediums, and crowds of visitors came to witness the remarkable materializations which occurred in their presence. Among these visitors was Madame Blavatsky, and, shortly after her, arrived Colonel H. S. Olcott—an apparently chance meeting, which was destined to have far-reaching effects. Their acquaintance grew into friendship, and Madame Blavatsky began to introduce to him some of the principles of the Eastern Wisdom in which she was versed.

Colonel Olcott writes that " a strange concatenation of events brought us together and united our lives for this work, under the superior direction of a group of Masters, especially of One, whose wise teaching, noble example, benevolent patience and paternal solicitude have made us regard Him with the reverence and love that a true Father inspires in his children. I am indebted to H. P. Blavatsky for making me know of the existence of these Masters and their Esoteric Philosophy ; and, later on, for acting as my mediator before I had come into direct personal intercourse with them.'

Colonel Henry Steele Olcott was an officer in the

American Army, who served in the war between North and South, and held an honourable position as a lawyer and writer. In him Madame Blavatsky, the teacher, found a colleague and organizer, who stood her in good stead in the following years, during which the Theosophical Society was born and commenced to develop.

In 1875, when it was formally founded, he was appointed its life-President, and for thirty-two years he filled that office with dignity, judgment and tact, winning the love of thousands by the sterling qualities of his heart and the noble work for humanity to which he set his hand.

CHAPTER V.

BIRTH OF THE THEOSOPHICAL SOCIETY.
1875-1878.

In starting the movement which was destined to do so much in breaking down the materialism of her epoch Madame Blavatsky first sought to interest those who were already aware of the phenomena of Spiritualism. Apparently her aim was to show that she could produce *at will* the phenomena with which many were becoming familiar in the séance room, and it would occupy too much space even to enumerate the wonders which she performed; those who knew her then have written fully of the world of marvel and magic in which she habitually moved at that time, yielding constantly to the demands for manifestation of her wonderful control over the unseen agencies in Nature, which waited upon her slightest wishes. It is not difficult to realize that by these means she speedily attracted the attention of a large circle of people, and this probably was the end she then had in view, for later on, when the Theosophical Society was established, she devoted herself to her true work as a Spiritual Teacher and refused to yield to the demand for " marvels."

The formation of a Society was proposed in the autumn of 1875; after some consideration its name was chosen, and at New York, on November 17th of that year, the President-Founder (Colonel Olcott) delivered his inaugural address. The original objects of the Society were not the three with which we are now familiar, but a much more elaborate and cumbersome series of seven rules ; on reading these through, however, one can trace the purpose, partially expressed, which Madame Blavatsky had in view, of bringing again to the world some of the Eastern Wisdom, and as the years passed the unnecessary and unsuitable objects fell away, until we find the three clearly defined " objects " of the Theosophical Society.

The progress of the new Society was very slow at first, indeed after a year's work, there survived only a good organization, a few somewhat indolent members, a certain notoriety and two friends, the Russian and the American who were in deadly earnest ; who never for a moment doubted the existence of their Masters, the excellence · of their mission, or its final success. The difficulties before them were enormous, but the following description of a visit paid by one of the Masters to Colonel Olcott may serve to show, on the other hand, the gracious encouragement given to the two comrades. One night Colonel Olcott was seated alone in his room quietly reading, when " all at once . . . there came a gleam of something white in the right-hand corner of my right eye ; I turned my head, dropped my book in astonishment and saw, towering above me in his great stature, an Oriental, clad in white garments, and wearing a headcloth or turban of amber striped fabric. . . . Long

raven hair hung from under his turban to the shoulders ;
. . . he was so grand a man, so imbued with the
majesty of moral strength, so luminously spiritual,
so evidently above the average humanity, that I felt
abashed in his presence, and bowed my head and
bent on my knee as one does before a god or a god-like
personage. A hand was lightly placed on my head,
a sweet though strong voice bade me be seated, and
when I raised my eyes, the Presence was seated in the
other chair beyond the table. He told me he had
come at the crisis when I needed him ; that my actions
had brought me to this point ; that it lay with me
alone whether he and I should meet again in this life
as co-workers for the good of mankind ; that a great
work was to be done for humanity and I had the right
to share in it if I wished ; that a mysterious tie, not
now to be explained to me, had drawn my colleague
and myself together ; a tie which could not be broken,
however strained it might be at times. . . . How
long he was there I cannot tell . . . but at last
he rose, I wondering at his great height, and observing
the sort of splendour in his countenance—not an
external shining, but the soft gleam, as it were, of an
inner light—that of the spirit, and . . . benig-
nantly saluting me in farewell, he was gone.

" To run and beat at H. P. B.'s door and tell her
my experience was the first natural impulse . . . I
returned to my room to think and the gray morning
found me still thinking and resolving. Out of those
thoughts and those resolves developed all my subsequent theosophical activities, and that loyalty to the
Masters behind our movement which the rudest shocks

and the cruellest disillusioning have never shaken."*

In the summer of 1875, *Isis Unveiled* was commenced and 1877 saw it published. The account of the writing of it as given by Colonel Olcott, who worked with Madame Blavatsky on the book, is but one more link in a chain of marvels. With a reference library of scarcely one hundred volumes she yet produced a book which suggests the free use of a Museum. Whence did she get this knowledge? How did she produce such a book? Here are her own words on the matter: " During the long years of my absence from home, I have constantly studied and have learned certain things. But when I wrote *Isis* I wrote it so easily that it was certainly no labour, but a real pleasure . . . I never put to myself the question, ' Can I write on this subject?' . . . for whenever I write upon a subject I know little of I address myself to *Them* and one of Them inspires me." Again she writes, " I live in a kind of permanent enchantment, a life of visions and sights with open eyes and no trance whatever to deceive my senses. . . . For several years, in order not to forget what I have learned elsewhere, I have been made to have permanently before my eyes all that I need to see. Thus, night and day, the images of the past are ever marshalled before my inner eye. Slowly, and gliding silently, like images in an enchanted panorama, centuries appear before me . . . and every important, and often unimportant event . . . remains photographed in my mind as though impressed in indelible colours. . . . I certainly refuse point-

---

blank to attribute it to my own knowledge or memory, for I could never arrive alone at either such premisses or conclusions."

In 1878, it was decided that the Founders should journey to India ; the Society was beginning to spread, a branch having been formed in London, and a number of Indian members having been enrolled. Their steamer carried them first to London, whence they trans-shipped for Bombay, where a Head-quarters was soon established.

CHAPTER VI.

WORK IN INDIA.
1878-1884.

A bungalow in the native quarters of Bombay was chosen by the Founders for the Theosophical headquarters, and before many weeks had passed, their rooms were thronged daily with native visitors, eager to discuss religious questions with Madame Blavatsky and to hear her explanations of their own ancient Scriptures. It is surely a striking testimony to the value of Theosophy that it can help equally the followers of various faiths, for just as Hindus, Buddhists, Parsees and others flocked round Madame Blakatsvy, so, in the present day, do they gather round Mrs. Besant to hear her lectures, while many earnest Christians find the greatest possible help in her words and writings. Theosophy flows out from the Source of all Religions and so each Faith is benefited by its coming.

The early days in Bombay were not easy, for Madame Blavatsky arrived in India with many misconceptions as to the British administration of India, and made no efforts to be introduced into European Society. Being a Russian, and moving solely among the natives, it was not strange that the police grew a little suspicious as to her motives, fearing that she might be a secret agent of the Russian Government ; they accordingly annoyed her exceedingly by setting a detective to watch her movements. This was done in such a very obvious and clumsy way and was such an absurd proceeding, that the unfortunate detective led an unhappy life, and in a very short time no more was heard or thought of the Russian spy scare.

The early days of the Society, like the olden days when the world was young, were made happy by the frequent appearances and help of the great Founders whom Madame Blavatsky served. Thus, as Colonel Olcott tells us, at Bombay, in their peaceful retreat, he and Madame Blavatsky were visited in person by the Teachers and made to realize more strongly than ever that they were not alone in their work, but were being watched and aided at every turn.

One very important step was taken shortly after their arrival in India. Mr. A. P. Sinnett, then editor of the *Pioneer*, the principal Anglo-Indian newspaper, wrote asking for information about their objects and for an introduction to Madame Blavatsky. Mr. Sinnett's interest in the movement at this very early stage was of great value, for he was in touch with, and highly respected by, the best Anglo-Indian Society. The first meetings were not immediately satisfactory, owing, doubtless, to the peculiarities of her disposition, but enough ground was gone over to show that Madame Blavatsky was the possessor of, or in touch with, great stores of occult learning, and many demonstrations were given of her possession of wonderful psychic powers. During a visit which the two Founders paid to Mr. and Mrs. Sinnett at Simla there occurred the remarkable events recorded in *The Occult World*—the first book which Mr. Sinnett contributed to the library of Theosophical literature.

Before long Mr. Sinnett saw through the outer peculiarities of Madame Blavatsky's temperament, and realized, as he himself has put it, " the splendour of her psychic gifts, her indomitable courage, which carried her through overwhelming dangers of all kinds, and her spiritual enthusiasm, which made all suffering and toil as dust in the balance compared with her allegiance to her unseen Masters." Through her he himself was given the privilege of communicating with the Masters, from Whom he received the letters upon which to base his work *Esoteric Buddhism*, the first book which gave any clear and orderly presentation of Theosophy.

Their sphere of influence extended so rapidly, and they were so overwhelmed by correspondence, that the Founders decided to start a magazine, as an organ through which to speak. Accordingly, in October, 1879, the *Theosophist* was launched, and paid its way from the first.

The Founders visited many places in India, establishing branches wherever they went and arousing public interest in their work ; everywhere they sought to inspire the true spirit of patriotism among the natives, by explaining to them the beauty and dignity of their own religions and the greatness of their ancient nation ; in Ceylon, which was also visited, they were enthusiastically welcomed, for the people saw in them the first European champions of Buddhism. Leaving the steamer which conveyed them to Colombo, Col. Olcott writes, " We embarked in a large boat, decorated with plantain trees and lines of bright coloured flowers, on which were the leading Buddhists of the place.

. . . on the jetty and on the beach a huge crowd awaited us, and rent the air with the united shout of ' Sadhoo, Sadhoo.' A white cloth was spread for us from the jetty steps to the road, where carriages were ready, and a thousand flags were frantically waved in welcome. . . . The roads were blocked with people and our progress was very slow. At the house three Chief Priests received and blessed us at the threshold, reciting appropriate Pâli verses. Then we had a levée and innumerable introductions ; the common people crowding every approach, filling every door and gazing through every window. This went on all day, to our great annoyance, for we could not get a breath of fresh air, but it was all so strong a proof of friendliness that we put up with it as best we could.
. . . Every now and then a new procession of yellow-robed monks, arranged in order of seniority of ordination, and each carrying his palm leaf fan, came to visit and bless us. It was an intoxicating experience altogether, a splendid augury of our future relations with the nation."*

It was during these long and fatiguing tours with Madame Blavatsky that Colonel Olcott commenced the wonderful series of cures by mesmeric passes for which he became famous throughout India. This fame became almost a nuisance, because at every town or village at which they stayed the Colonel was literally besieged by applicants suffering from all sorts of pains and troubles. An incident which occurred at Tinnevelly is typical and well worth quoting. " I had gone to the Pagoda," Colonel Olcott writes, " and was

---

followed by at least a thousand idlers, who, for lack of better amusement, watched my every step, and exchanged opinions on my personal appearance. A young man of twenty-five or thirty was brought to me through the press, by his father, with a prayer that I would restore his speech which he had lost three years before. Having neither elbow-room nor breathing space, I climbed up on the continuous pedestal or basement that supports a long line of monolithic carved figures of Hindu deities, drew the patient up after me, called for silence and made the father tell the people about the case." Then the Colonel laid his hands on the unfortunate dumb man and made seven circular passes on the head, and seven long passes, and in less than five minutes speech was restored, and the Colonel made the young man shout at the top of his voice the names of Hindu deities. A scene of intense enthusiasm followed.

In the midst of all this activity a house-boat journey made by the Founders, with some colleagues, came as a welcome change. Madame Blavatsky was in good health and spirits, and the quiet days of restful voyaging through the country, silent, save when passing an occasional town, must have been very refreshing to the two Pioneers. Their hopes at this time in regard to the future of the work on which they were engaged, were not so much that a strong and wide-spreading society might be formed, but rather that Theosophical ideas might gradually colour and influence modern thought and opinion. Comparatively old people as they were, they could scarcely have hoped to build up the wide-branching Society which they nevertheless succeeded in developing in the next ten years.

The latter end of 1882 was marked by the grave illness of Madame Blavatsky at Bombay. The strain of constant labour, travelling and misrepresentation, and her natural excitability of temperament combined to bring about a collapse. She was directed to go north *via* Darjeeling to meet her Occult Guardians, and although she only spent two or three days with them she returned practically well again.

In their wanderings in India the Founders had always kept a look-out for a suitable home for the Society; at the end of 1882 they came upon just the place they wanted. This was at Adyar, a suburb of Madras, where they saw and purchased the property which is now so well-known as the Head-quarters of the Theosophical Society and the home of its President.

COLONEL H. S. OLCOTT.

(To face p. 49.)

CHAPTER VII.

WORK IN EUROPE.
1884-1887.

After the illness and sudden cure referred to in our last chapter it was decided that Madame Blavatsky should take a trip to Europe, to try to establish herself in health again, and at the last moment Colonel Olcott joined her. She went to Naples first, and then to Paris, where she met many Theosophists from all parts of Europe and from America, and also some of her own Russian relatives. Countess Wachtmeister, who met her then for the first time, gives some very interesting descriptions of those days, when many celebrated men and women gathered round her to listen to and join in her conversation, and, perchance, to witness some of the remarkable phenomena which so frequently occurred in her presence. Of H. P. B. (as her pupils came to call her) at this time, the Countess writes that "her features were instinct with power, and expressed an innate nobility of character that more than filled the anticipations I had formed ; but what chiefly arrested my attention was the steady gaze of her wonderful grey eyes, piercing yet calm and inscrutable ; they shone with a serene light which seemed to penetrate and unveil the secrets of the heart." H. P. B. the teacher, occultist and philosopher of later years, supported by a devoted band of loyal pupils, was a finer character than the impetuous and

D

excitable Russian of former days; but rather than a mere feeling of wonder at this should we not be moved to deeper love and reverence for one who was strong enough to overcome the difficulties *within* herself as well as those which thronged her path in the world without?

H. P. B. crossed to London in the summer of 1884, and attracted a great deal of attention to herself and to the movement she served. A few of our oldest English members joined the Society during this visit and a larger number during the last three years of her life (1888-1891), which were spent in London.

One of the greatest trials and sorrows of her life of which we must now speak fell upon her during this first London visit. Readers will remember that she met a certain Madame Coulomb and her husband in Cairo, long before the Theosophical Society was founded, and that she felt herself under a certain obligation to them because of some little assistance they gave her while she was waiting for money to reach her from Russia. Later on these two people came to her in Bombay, where they were stranded, penniless and in great difficulties, and H. P. B. took them into her own household, where they were given the posts of stewards, looking after household matters and living in comfort. They were maintained in their positions at Adyar when the head-quarters were removed there, but, unhappily, Madame Coulomb's former affection for Madame Blavatsky suffered a sea-change and she became her enemy, seeking to injure H. P. B. in any way she could. Her opportunity came when H. P. B. left India for Europe.

The whole trouble centred round the phenomena which H. P. B. had so lavishly displayed. Madame Coulomb supplied to the Editor of a Christian magazine at Madras a series of letters, purporting to have been written to her by Madame Blavatsky, which, if genuine, would have shown her to have employed Madame Coulomb and her husband as confederates in producing some of these phenomena. They further supported their case by showing Madame Blavatsky's room at Adyar, in which was found a clumsy arrangement of sliding-panels, etc., by means of which, they alleged, the wonders had been worked. I have no space in which to go into details regarding these charges, but I am glad and proud to say (as other members of the Society must be) that one of the first acts, after her election, of our new President, Mrs. Besant, was to publish a full and complete defence of H. P. B.*   H. P. B. at once denied that the letters had ever been written by her, but, to their shame, be it said, those who accused her never even allowed her to see them ! While, with regard to the sliding panels, etc., Mrs. Besant, shows conclusively, from the testimony of many who were on the spot, that these must have been put up *after* Madame Blavatsky left Adyar for Europe, and while the Coulombs, as house-keepers, had charge of the establishment.

It was long, however, before a full and correct account of these occurrences was obtainable, and in the meantime a great blow had been dealt at the

---

* *H.P.B. and the Masters of Wisdom.* Annie Besant. (London, Theosophical Publishing Society.)

Theosophical Movement, which well-nigh crushed it. On Madame Blavatsky, of course, fell the brunt of the storm and the suffering. Only a few of her friends in the West were faithful to her, but in the East, where Madame Blavatsky returned for a brief visit, the majority of the members stood by her. Her health, however, completely broke down again and she returned to Europe.

Out of misfortunes, however, some good speedily began to come. In the days of enforced quiet, while the work seemed stunned by the blow which had fallen upon it and the disturbances which followed, the fountain of the Ancient Wisdom began to flow more fully than ever before for H. P. B., and she felt that by her writings she might justify herself and draw the Movement together. She was right, for her writings from that time to her death are those by which her memory will live and the Society will grow.

Reminiscences of Madame Blavatsky, by Countess Wachtmeister, now furnishes us with accounts of the next few years of H. P. B.'s life in Europe. At the end of 1885, the Countess went to live with Madame Blavatsky at Würzburg, learning that she was in need of care and companionship. The following description of a single day will serve to indicate the routine of her life at this time. By seven in the morning Madame Blavatsky was at her desk writing, with only a pause for breakfast, until one o'clock, when sometimes she would stop for dinner, but at other times her door would remain closed for hours longer, to the despair of the maid, who bemoaned the spoilt food. At seven o'clock writing was laid aside and the rest of the evening was spent pleasantly with the Countess until nine, when H. P. B. went to bed, where she would surround herself with her Russian newspapers and read them till a late hour.

The work on which Madame Blavatsky was engaged at this time was the *Secret Doctrine*, the writing of which was a long and arduous labour, requiring the greatest possible freedom from distractions of any kind. As with *Isis Unveiled*, Madame Blavatsky was constantly helped in this work by the Masters, who dictated to her, wrote for her occasionally, or showed her ancient events and scenes, descriptions of which were required. As in the former work, quotations and references were made to books which Madame Blavatsky had not and could not have had at hand. But indeed the only way to gain an idea of the greatness of this work is to read it. In it, for the first time, are translated stanzas from the mysterious *Book of Dzyan*, which contains the record of the life-history of our earth and the system to which we belong, since its birth, myriads of years ago. Only the eye of a seer can understand and translate into speech this record ; Madame Blavatsky did so translate parts of it and added to it commentaries and explanations of her own and other people's, and as a result we have in the *Secret Doctrine* perhaps the grandest picture of evolution ever penned. But the strenuous work involved in the production of the *Secret Doctrine*—a work which kept Madame Blavatsky chained to her desk week-in and week-out with scarcely a break for out-door exercise—told very heavily on her health. She moved from Würzburg to Ostend, whither Countess

Wachtmeister accompanied her. Matters grew worse
there, and two doctors had to be called in ; they held
out no hope of recovery and only marvelled that
H. P. B. had lived so long with the complicated dis-
orders from which she suffered. One night matters
reached a crisis ; H. P. B. herself thought that the
time had come for her to lay down her body, and told
the Countess, who was sitting up with her, how glad
she was at the prospect of being free from so worn-out
an instrument, although she had hoped to give more
to the world. At last she dropped off into a state of
unconsciousness, and the Countess gave herself over
to sad reflections as to the apparent uselessness of all
Madame Blavatsky's self-sacrifice and suffering, for
the work seemed too weak to continue without her,
who was the very life-blood of it. At last worn out
with the inevitable fatigues of nursing and her own
sorrowful thoughts, the Countess herself sank into
unconsciousness.

"When I opened my eyes," she writes, " the early
morning light was stealing in, and a dire apprehension
came over me that I had slept, and that perhaps
H. P. B. had died during my sleep. . . . I turned
round towards the bed in horror and there I saw
H. P. B. looking at me calmly with her clear, grey eyes,
as she said, ' Countess, come here.' I flew to her side.
' What has happened, H. P. B., you look so different
from what you did last night ? ' She replied, ' Yes,
Master has been here ; He gave me my choice, that I
might die, and be free if I would, or I might live and
finish the *Secret Doctrino*. He told me how great
would be my sufferings, and what a terrible time I

1890.

(To face p. 55.)

would have before me in England (for I am to go there) ; but when I thought of those students to whom I shall be permitted to teach a few things, and of the Theosophical Society in general, to which I have already given my heart's blood, I accepted the sacrifice,' "— and there are many now in England and abroad who bless her every day of their lives for this sacrifice which brought Theosophy to them when they might never otherwise have heard of it.

CHAPTER VIII.

WORK IN ENGLAND, 1887-1891.

The grave illness at Ostend, from which Madame
Blavatsky so marvellously recovered, was followed by
four years of strenuous work in London—work which
formed the foundation for many of our well-established
activities. The *Secret Doctrine* was gradually completed and finally published ; it stands alone in our
literature, head and shoulders above any other books
we have, a veritable mine to which the student may
return over and over again and always find something
new and precious. Then H. P. B. translated the *Voice
of the Silence*, a book which comes from early Buddhist
days and which mellows the wisdom of its words by
that atmosphere of compassion which is so characteristic of the Buddha's teaching. The *Key to Theosophy*
was also written, and *Lucifer*, now known as the
Theosophical Review, was started and edited by H. P. B.
for nearly four years. Besides these literary activities,
and owing to the stimulus of her presence, the whole
of the movement in England, which had been confined
almost entirely to London, grew and flourished exceedingly.

This was a wonderful record of work to be done
with such a worn-out body ; but in addition to it
H. P. B. continued the perhaps still more important
task of training pupils, so that the movement might
be carried on when she left. The Blavatsky Lodge

was formed, and before long a wide circle of pupils and sympathisers gathered round her, amongst whom were some of the best of our English workers.

On first coming to London a house in Norwood was taken, but it was soon found too small and inconvenient, and a move was made to Lansdowne Road, where a larger house was taken. Madame Blavatsky occupied rooms on the ground floor ; for twelve hours a day she would work at her desk, and in the evening would receive visitors—strangely varied visitors they were too ; well-known men of science, learned professors, literary men, agnostics and socialists, artists, all finding something of attraction in this wonderful Russian woman whose profound knowledge commanded attention and respect. On Thursday evenings she would be present at the meeting of the Blavatsky Lodge and answer questions in elucidation of different points in her writings.

Among these visitors came Mrs. Besant, to whom the *Secret Doctrine* had been given for review. She wrote asking for an interview with Madame Blavatsky, and in due course presented herself at the door of 17, Lansdowne Road. Mrs. Besant writes " A pause, a " swift passing through hall and outer room and folding- " doors thrown back, a figure in a large chair before " a table, a voice, vibrant, compelling: 'My dear Mrs. " Besant, I have so long wished to see you,' and I " was standing with my hand in her firm grip, and " looking for the first time in this life straight into the " eyes of ' H. P. Blavatsky.' I was conscious of a " sudden leaping forth of my heart—was it a recog- " nition ?—and then, I am ashamed to say, a fierce

" rebellion, a fierce withdrawal, as of some wild animal
" when it feels a mastering hand. I sat down, after
" some introductions that conveyed no ideas to me,
" and listened. She talked of travels, of various
" countries, easy brilliant talk, her eyes veiled, her
" exquisitely moulded fingers rolling cigarettes inces-
" santly. Nothing special to record, no word of
" occultism, nothing mysterious, a woman of the
" world chatting with her evening visitors. We rose
" to go, and for a moment the veil lifted, and two
" brilliant, piercing eyes met mine, and with a yearning
" throb in the voice : ' Oh my dear Mrs. Besant, if
" you would only come among us ! '   I felt a well-
" nigh uncontrollable desire to bend down and kiss
" her, under the compulsion of that yearning voice,
" those compelling eyes, but with a flash of the old
" unbending pride and an inward jeer at my own folly,
" I said a commonplace polite good-bye, and turned
" away with some inanely courteous and evasive
" remark. ' Child,' she said to me long afterwards,
" 'your pride is terrible; you are as proud as Lucifer
" himself.'   But truly I think I never showed it to her
" again after that first evening, though it sprang up
" wrathfully in her defence many and many a time,
" until I learned the pettiness and the worthlessness
" of all criticism, and knew that the blind were objects
" of compassion, not of scorn."

Before long Lansdowne Road was outgrown and a
move was made at Mrs. Besant's invitation to her
house in Avenue Road. A lecture hall was built
beside the house and No. 19, Avenue Road, became
the head-quarters of the Society in London for a dozen

years, until it was moved nearer the centre of London.

Avenue Road was the last home of the body known as Madame Blavatsky, for here, on May 8th, 1891, it was laid aside finally, but not until the movement in England had been placed on a firm footing and pupils had been found to carry on the work to which she had devoted her life. " Endurance and patience," says Mrs. Besant, " have certainly been the crowning qualities of H. P. B. as I have known her during the last years of her life. . . . The most salient of her characteristics was implied in these crowning qualities ; it was that of strength, steady strength, unyielding as a rock. I have seen weaklings dash themselves up against her and then whimper that she was hard ; but I have also seen her face to face with a woman who had been her cruel enemy, but who was in distress, and every feature was radiant with a divine compassion which only did not forgive because it would not admit that it had been outraged."

H. P. B. was in a very real sense the mother of the Theosophical Society ; the seeds of Spiritual Truth which she came to sow required tender care and protection ere they could sprout and grow into healthy plants, and that fostering care she gave, taking upon herself all the storm and stress, so that within this shell there might be peace. Every spiritual movement seems to be mothered in this way by some great Soul who walls it round with shielding arms, in its early stages, and breathes into it the living warmth of Spiritual Life. As a mother gives her life to a child, so did H. P. B. identify her life with that of her child —the Society she founded—and we who belong to it, although we may not have seen H. P. B. in this life, should ever think of her in this way. H. P. B. is as much as ever a beneficent power in the Theosophical movement, and by keeping her memory green we shall be more likely to know her when she takes up her work again on the physical plane in years to come ; in the meantime we have all, even the youngest of us, work for Theosophy that we can do, whether by thought or by word or by action, and one of our motives for doing it loyally and as well as we can, might very well be that when H. P. B. *does* come back, the Theosophical movement may be strong and healthy and ready for the Leader.

The Theosophical Society.

OBJECTS.

To form a nucleus of the universal Brotherhood of Humanity, without distinction of race, creed, sex, caste, or colour.

To encourage the study of comparative religion, philosophy, and science.

To investigate unexplained laws of nature and the powers latent in man.

Any person desiring information as to the Theosophical Society is invited to communicate with the General Secretary, Theosophical Society, London.

THE THEOSOPHICAL SOCIETY is composed of students, belonging to any religion in the world or to none, who are united by their approval of the above objects, by their wish to remove religious antagonisms and to draw together men of good-will whatsoever their religious opinions, and by their desire to study religious truths and to share the results of their studies with others. Their bond of union is not the profession of a common belief, but a common search and aspiration for Truth. They hold that Truth should be sought by study, by reflection, by purity of life, by devotion to high ideals, and they regard Truth as a prize to be striven for, not as a dogma to be imposed by authority. They consider that belief should be the result of individual study or intuition, and not its antecedent, and should rest on knowledge, not on assertion. They extend tolerance to all, even to the intolerant, not as a privilege they bestow, but as a duty they perform, and they seek to remove ignorance, not to punish it. They see every religion as an expression of the DIVINE WISDOM, and prefer its study to its condemnation, and its practice to proselytism. Peace is their watch-word, as Truth is their aim.

Of Heaven and Earth: Essays Presented at the First Sitchin Studies Day, edited by Zecharia Sitchin. ISBN 1-885395-17-5 • 164 pages • 5 1/2 x 8 1/2 • trade paper • illustrated • $14.95

God Games: What Do You Do Forever?, by Neil Freer. ISBN 1-885395-39-6 • 312 pages • 6 x 9 • trade paper • $19.95

Space Travelers and the Genesis of the Human Form: Evidence of Intelligent Contact in the Solar System, by Joan d'Arc. ISBN 1-58509-127-8 • 208 pages • 6 x 9 • trade paper • illustrated • $18.95

Humanity's Extraterrestrial Origins: ET Influences on Humankind's Biological and Cultural Evolution, by Dr. Arthur David Horn with Lynette Mallory-Horn. ISBN 3-931652-31-9 • 373 pages • 6 x 9 • trade paper • $17.00

Past Shock: The Origin of Religion and Its Impact on the Human Soul, by Jack Barranger. ISBN 1-885395-08-6 • 126 pages • 6 x 9 • trade paper • illustrated • $12.95

Flying Serpents and Dragons: The Story of Mankind's Reptilian Past, by R.A. Boulay. ISBN 1-885395-38-8 • 276 pages • 6 x 9 • trade paper • illustrated • $19.95

Triumph of the Human Spirit: The Greatest Achievements of the Human Soul and How Its Power Can Change Your Life, by Paul Tice. ISBN 1-885395-57-4 • 295 pages • 6 x 9 • trade paper • illustrated • $19.95

Mysteries Explored: The Search for Human Origins, UFOs, and Religious Beginnings, by Jack Barranger and Paul Tice. ISBN 1-58509-101-4 • 104 pages • 6 x 9 • trade paper • $12.95

Mushrooms and Mankind: The Impact of Mushrooms on Human Consciousness and Religion, by James Arthur. ISBN 1-58509-151-0 • 180 pages • 6 x 9 • trade paper • $16.95

Vril or Vital Magnetism, with an Introduction by Paul Tice. ISBN 1-58509-030-1 • 124 pages • 5 1/2 x 8 1/2 • trade paper • $12.95

The Odic Force: Letters on Od and Magnetism, by Karl von Reichenbach. ISBN 1-58509-001-8 • 192 pages • 6 x 9 • trade paper • $15.95

The New Revelation: The Coming of a New Spiritual Paradigm, by Arthur Conan Doyle. ISBN 1-58509-220-7 • 124 pages • 6 x 9 • trade paper • $12.95

The Astral World: Its Scenes, Dwellers, and Phenomena, by Swami Panchadasi. ISBN 1-58509-071-9 • 104 pages • 6 x 9 • trade paper • $11.95

Reason and Belief: The Impact of Scientific Discovery on Religious and Spiritual Faith, by Sir Oliver Lodge. ISBN 1-58509-226-6 • 180 pages • 6 x 9 • trade paper • $17.95

William Blake: A Biography, by Basil De Selincourt. ISBN 1-58509-225-8 • 384 pages • 6 x 9 • trade paper • $28.95

The Divine Pymander: And Other Writings of Hermes Trismegistus, translated by John D. Chambers. ISBN 1-58509-046-8 • 196 pages • 6 x 9 • trade paper • $16.95

Theosophy and The Secret Doctrine, by Harriet L. Henderson. Includes **H.P. Blavatsky: An Outline of Her Life,** by Herbert Whyte, ISBN 1-58509-075-1 • 132 pages • 6 x 9 • trade paper • $13.95

The Light of Egypt, Volume One: The Science of the Soul and the Stars, by Thomas H. Burgoyne. ISBN 1-58509-051-4 • 320 pages • 6 x 9 • trade paper • illustrated • $24.95

The Light of Egypt, Volume Two: The Science of the Soul and the Stars, by Thomas H. Burgoyne. ISBN 1-58509-052-2 • 224 pages • 6 x 9 • trade paper • illustrated • $17.95

The Jumping Frog and 18 Other Stories: 19 Unforgettable Mark Twain Stories, by Mark Twain. ISBN 1-58509-200-2 • 128 pages • 6 x 9 • trade paper • $12.95

The Devil's Dictionary: A Guidebook for Cynics, by Ambrose Bierce. ISBN 1-58509-016-6 • 144 pages • 6 x 9 • trade paper • $12.95

The Smoky God: Or The Voyage to the Inner World, by Willis George Emerson. ISBN 1-58509-067-0 • 184 pages • 6 x 9 • trade paper • illustrated • $15.95

A Short History of the World, by H.G. Wells. ISBN 1-58509-211-8 • 320 pages • 6 x 9 • trade paper • $24.95

The Voyages and Discoveries of the Companions of Columbus, by Washington Irving. ISBN 1-58509-500-1 • 352 pages • 6 x 9 • hard cover • $39.95

History of Baalbek, by Michel Alouf. ISBN 1-58509-063-8 • 196 pages • 5 x 8 • trade paper • illustrated • $15.95

Ancient Egyptian Masonry: The Building Craft, by Sommers Clarke and R. Engelback. ISBN 1-58509-059-X • 350 pages • 6 x 9 • trade paper • illustrated • $26.95

That Old Time Religion: The Story of Religious Foundations, by Jordan Maxwell and Paul Tice. ISBN 1-58509-100-6 • 220 pages • 6 x 9 • trade paper • $19.95

Jumpin' Jehovah: Exposing the Atrocities of the Old Testament God, by Paul Tice. ISBN 1-58509-102-2 • 104 pages • 6 x 9 • trade paper • $12.95

The Book of Enoch: A Work of Visionary Revelation and Prophecy, Revealing Divine Secrets and Fantastic Information about Creation, Salvation, Heaven and Hell, translated by R. H. Charles. ISBN 1-58509-019-0 • 152 pages • 5 1/2 x 8 1/2 • trade paper • $13.95

The Book of Enoch: Translated from the Editor's Ethiopic Text and Edited with an Enlarged Introduction, Notes and Indexes, Together with a Reprint of the Greek Fragments, edited by R. H. Charles. ISBN 1-58509-080-8 • 448 pages • 6 x 9 • trade paper • $34.95

The Book of the Secrets of Enoch, translated from the Slavonic by W. R. Morfill. Edited, with Introduction and Notes by R. H. Charles. ISBN 1-58509-020-4 • 148 pages • 5 1/2 x 8 1/2 • trade paper • $13.95

Enuma Elish: The Seven Tablets of Creation, Volume One, by L. W. King. ISBN 1-58509-041-7 • 236 pages • 6 x 9 • trade paper • illustrated • $18.95

Enuma Elish: The Seven Tablets of Creation, Volume Two, by L. W. King. ISBN 1-58509-042-5 • 260 pages • 6 x 9 • trade paper • illustrated • $19.95

Enuma Elish, Volumes One and Two: The Seven Tablets of Creation, by L. W. King. Two volumes from above bound as one. ISBN 1-58509-043-3 • 496 pages • 6 x 9 • trade paper • illustrated • $38.90

The Archko Volume: Documents that Claim Proof to the Life, Death, and Resurrection of Christ, by Drs. McIntosh and Twyman. ISBN 1-58509-082-4 • 248 pages • 6 x 9 • trade paper • $20.95

The Lost Language of Symbolism: An Inquiry into the Origin of Certain Letters, Words, Names, Fairy-Tales, Folklore, and Mythologies, by Harold Bayley. ISBN 1-58509-070-0 • 384 pages • 6 x 9 • trade paper • $27.95

The Book of Jasher: A Suppressed Book that was Removed from the Bible, Referred to in Joshua and Second Samuel, translated by Albinus Alcuin (800 AD). ISBN 1-58509-081-6 • 304 pages • 6 x 9 • trade paper • $24.95

The Bible's Most Embarrassing Moments, with an Introduction by Paul Tice. ISBN 1-58509-025-5 • 172 pages • 5 x 8 • trade paper • $14.95

History of the Cross: The Pagan Origin and Idolatrous Adoption and Worship of the Image, by Henry Dana Ward. ISBN 1-58509-056-5 • 104 pages • 6 x 9 • trade paper • illustrated • $11.95

Was Jesus Influenced by Buddhism? A Comparative Study of the Lives and Thoughts of Gautama and Jesus, by Dwight Goddard. ISBN 1-58509-027-1 • 252 pages • 6 x 9 • trade paper • $19.95

History of the Christian Religion to the Year Two Hundred, by Charles B. Waite. ISBN 1-885395-15-9 • 556 pages. • 6 x 9 • hard cover • $25.00

Symbols, Sex, and the Stars, by Ernest Busenbark. ISBN 1-885395-19-1 • 396 pages • 5 1/2 x 8 1/2 • trade paper • $22.95

History of the First Council of Nice: A World's Christian Convention, A.D. 325, by Dean Dudley. ISBN 1-58509-023-9 • 132 pages • 5 1/2 x 8 1/2 • trade paper • $12.95

The World's Sixteen Crucified Saviors, by Kersey Graves. ISBN 1-58509-018-2 • 436 pages • 5 1/2 x 8 1/2 • trade paper • $29.95

Babylonian Influence on the Bible and Popular Beliefs: A Comparative Study of Genesis I.2, by A. Smythe Palmer. ISBN 1-58509-000-X • 124 pages • 6 x 9 • trade paper • $12.95

Biography of Satan: Exposing the Origins of the Devil, by Kersey Graves. ISBN 1-885395-11-6 • 168 pages • 5 1/2 x 8 1/2 • trade paper • $13.95

The Malleus Maleficarum: The Notorious Handbook Once Used to Condemn and Punish "Witches", by Heinrich Kramer and James Sprenger. ISBN 1-58509-098-0 • 332 pages • 6 x 9 • trade paper • $25.95

Crux Ansata: An Indictment of the Roman Catholic Church, by H. G. Wells. ISBN 1-58509-210-X • 160 pages • 6 x 9 • trade paper • $14.95

Emanuel Swedenborg: The Spiritual Columbus, by U.S.E. (William Spear). ISBN 1-58509-096-4 • 208 pages • 6 x 9 • trade paper • $17.95

Dragons and Dragon Lore, by Ernest Ingersoll. ISBN 1-58509-021-2 • 228 pages • 6 x 9 • trade paper • illustrated • $17.95

The Vision of God, by Nicholas of Cusa. ISBN 1-58509-004-2 • 160 pages • 5 x 8 • trade paper • $13.95

The Historical Jesus and the Mythical Christ: Separating Fact From Fiction, by Gerald Massey. ISBN 1-58509-073-5 • 244 pages • 6 x 9 • trade paper • $18.95

Gog and Magog: The Giants in Guildhall; Their Real and Legendary History, with an Account of Other Giants at Home and Abroad, by F.W. Fairholt. ISBN 1-58509-084-0 • 172 pages • 6 x 9 • trade paper • $16.95

The Origin and Evolution of Religion, by Albert Churchward. ISBN 1-58509-078-6 • 504 pages • 6 x 9 • trade paper • $39.95

The Origin of Biblical Traditions, by Albert T. Clay. ISBN 1-58509-065-4 • 220 pages • 5 1/2 x 8 1/2 • trade paper • $17.95

Aryan Sun Myths, by Sarah Elizabeth Titcomb, Introduction by Charles Morris. ISBN 1-58509-069-7 • 192 pages • 6 x 9 • trade paper • $15.95

The Social Record of Christianity, by Joseph McCabe. Includes *The Lies and Fallacies of the Encyclopedia Britannica,* ISBN 1-58509-215-0 • 204 pages • 6 x 9 • trade paper • $17.95

The History of the Christian Religion and Church During the First Three Centuries, by Dr. Augustus Neander. ISBN 1-58509-077-8 • 112 pages • 6 x 9 • trade paper • $12.95

Ancient Symbol Worship: Influence of the Phallic Idea in the Religions of Antiquity, by Hodder M. Westropp and C. Staniland Wake. ISBN 1-58509-048-4 • 120 pages • 6 x 9 • trade paper • illustrated • $12.95

The Gnosis: Or Ancient Wisdom in the Christian Scriptures, by William Kingsland. ISBN 1-58509-047-6 • 232 pages • 6 x 9 • trade paper • $18.95

The Evolution of the Idea of God: An Inquiry into the Origin of Religions, by Grant Allen. ISBN 1-58509-074-3 • 160 pages • 6 x 9 • trade paper • $14.95

Sun Lore of All Ages: A Survey of Solar Mythology, Folklore, Customs, Worship, Festivals, and Superstition, by William Tyler Olcott. ISBN 1-58509-044-1 • 316 pages • 6 x 9 • trade paper • $24.95

Nature Worship: An Account of Phallic Faiths and Practices Ancient and Modern, by the Author of Phallicism with an Introduction by Tedd St. Rain. ISBN 1-58509-049-2 • 112 pages • 6 x 9 • trade paper • illustrated • $12.95

Life and Religion, by Max Muller. ISBN 1-885395-10-8 • 237 pages • 5 1/2 x 8 1/2 • trade paper • $14.95

Jesus: God, Man, or Myth? An Examination of the Evidence, by Herbert Cutner. ISBN 1-58509-072-7 • 304 pages • 6 x 9 • trade paper • $23.95

Pagan and Christian Creeds: Their Origin and Meaning, by Edward Carpenter. ISBN 1-58509-024-7 • 316 pages • 5 1/2 x 8 1/2 • trade paper • $24.95

The Christ Myth: A Study, by Elizabeth Evans. ISBN 1-58509-037-9 • 136 pages • 6 x 9 • trade paper • $13.95

Popery: Foe of the Church and the Republic, by Joseph F. Van Dyke. ISBN 1-58509-058-1 • 336 pages • 6 x 9 • trade paper • illustrated • $25.95

Career of Religious Ideas, by Hudson Tuttle. ISBN 1-58509-066-2 • 172 pages • 5 x 8 • trade paper • $15.95

Buddhist Suttas: Major Scriptural Writings from Early Buddhism, by T.W. Rhys Davids. ISBN 1-58509-079-4 • 376 pages • 6 x 9 • trade paper • $27.95

Early Buddhism, by T. W. Rhys Davids. Includes **Buddhist Ethics: The Way to Salvation?,** by Paul Tice. ISBN 1-58509-076-X • 112 pages • 6 x 9 • trade paper • $12.95

The Fountain-Head of Religion: A Comparative Study of the Principal Religions of the World and a Manifestation of their Common Origin from the Vedas, by Ganga Prasad. ISBN 1-58509-054-9 • 276 pages • 6 x 9 • trade paper • $22.95

India: What Can It Teach Us?, by Max Muller. ISBN 1-58509-064-6 • 284 pages • 5 1/2 x 8 1/2 • trade paper • $22.95

Matrix of Power: How the World has Been Controlled by Powerful People Without Your Knowledge, by Jordan Maxwell. ISBN 1-58509-120-0 • 104 pages • 6 x 9 • trade paper • $12.95

Cyberculture Counterconspiracy: A Steamshovel Web Reader, Volume One, edited by Kenn Thomas. ISBN 1-58509-125-1 • 180 pages • 6 x 9 • trade paper • illustrated • $16.95

Cyberculture Counterconspiracy: A Steamshovel Web Reader, Volume Two, edited by Kenn Thomas. ISBN 1-58509-126-X • 132 pages • 6 x 9 • trade paper • illustrated • $13.95

Oklahoma City Bombing: The Suppressed Truth, by Jon Rappoport. ISBN 1-885395-22-1 • 112 pages • 5 1/2 x 8 1/2 • trade paper • $12.95

The Protocols of the Learned Elders of Zion, by Victor Marsden. ISBN 1-58509-015-8 • 312 pages • 6 x 9 • trade paper • $24.95

Secret Societies and Subversive Movements, by Nesta H. Webster. ISBN 1-58509-092-1 • 432 pages • 6 x 9 • trade paper • $29.95

The Secret Doctrine of the Rosicrucians, by Magus Incognito. ISBN 1-58509-091-3 • 256 pages • 6 x 9 • trade paper • $20.95

The Origin and Evolution of Freemasonry: Connected with the Origin and Evolution of the Human Race, by Albert Churchward. ISBN 1-58509-029-8 • 240 pages • 6 x 9 • trade paper • $18.95

The Lost Key: An Explanation and Application of Masonic Symbols, by Prentiss Tucker. ISBN 1-58509-050-6 • 192 pages • 6 x 9 • trade paper • illustrated • $15.95

The Character, Claims, and Practical Workings of Freemasonry, by Rev. C.G. Finney. ISBN 1-58509-094-8 • 288 pages • 6 x 9 • trade paper • $22.95

The Secret World Government or "The Hidden Hand": The Unrevealed in History, by Maj.-Gen., Count Cherep-Spiridovich. ISBN 1-58509-093-X • 270 pages • 6 x 9 • trade paper • $21.95

The Magus, Book One: A Complete System of Occult Philosophy, by Francis Barrett. ISBN 1-58509-031-X • 200 pages • 6 x 9 • trade paper • illustrated • $16.95

The Magus, Book Two: A Complete System of Occult Philosophy, by Francis Barrett. ISBN 1-58509-032-8 • 220 pages • 6 x 9 • trade paper • illustrated • $17.95

The Magus, Book One and Two: A Complete System of Occult Philosophy, by Francis Barrett. ISBN 1-58509-033-6 • 420 pages • 6 x 9 • trade paper • illustrated • $34.90

The Key of Solomon The King, by S. Liddell MacGregor Mathers. ISBN 1-58509-022-0 • 152 pages • 6 x 9 • trade paper • illustrated • $12.95

Magic and Mystery in Tibet, by Alexandra David-Neel. ISBN 1-58509-097-2 • 352 pages • 6 x 9 • trade paper • $26.95

The Comte de St. Germain, by I. Cooper Oakley. ISBN 1-58509-068-9 • 280 pages • 6 x 9 • trade paper • illustrated • $22.95

Alchemy Rediscovered and Restored, by A. Cockren. ISBN 1-58509-028-X • 156 pages • 5 1/2 x 8 1/2 • trade paper • $13.95

The 6th and 7th Books of Moses, with an Introduction by Paul Tice. ISBN 1-58509-045-X • 188 pages • 6 x 9 • trade paper • illustrated • $16.95

www.ingramcontent.com/pod-product-compliance
Lightning Source LLC
LaVergne TN
LVHW011403080426
835511LV00005B/392